MW00441167

A TAIL of LOVE

a Tail of Love

Life Lessons from Scrappy, a Pet Therapy Dog

LARRY N GROGAN

A Tail of Love: Life Lessons from Scrappy, a Pet Therapy Dog
© Copyright 2021 Larry N Grogan

For more information, email larrygrogan5@gmail.com

ISBN: 978-1-7379641-1-7

Dedication

A Tail of Love: Life Lessons from Scrappy, a Pet Therapy Dog is dedicated to Scrappy, the most incredible animal I have ever encountered. Scrappy's natural ability to exude love was so powerful it impacted the lives of most everyone she came in contact with. For Scrappy, love was a responsibility, as the first chapter of this book is so titled.

For all the good Scrappy provided in her lifetime as a pet therapy dog, there are many others who have done the same. Therefore, *A Tail of Love: Life Lessons from Scrappy, a Pet Therapy Dog is* also dedicated to all pet therapy animals, like Olive Oyl, who dedicated their lives to aid others.

May they get the rest they so deservedly earned, but also may they continue to give us the insight we need for our own lives through their memories.

Contents

Introduction

S unday, June 30, 2019, was the worst day of my life. I lost my friend, my companion, and a major portion of my identity.

I realized my selfishness at 3 am that morning and knew I had to let her go. She had given me twelve and a half years of joy, love, and fun, but sadly her soul was slipping away. It was time to end the pain and do the right thing for her. She had always done the right thing for me. As painful as it was, I was determined to make her last moments as memorable as possible.

We started at the park where she used to run endlessly—to the point of *my* exhaustion, not hers. Now, with her kidneys failing, it was difficult for her to even stand on the grass. We waited for the sun to rise before moving on.

From the park, we went to the Children's Hospital, where she comforted so many children, families, nurses, and doctors. After all,

Scrappy was a pet therapy dog, and her work was memorable, faithful, and with purpose. I carried Scrappy in my arms into the chapel.

I reflected on her incredible work at the hospital, but I went into the chapel to pray. To pray for her and for me.

I prayed that Scrappy would no longer feel pain, knowing my pain was only beginning. I thanked Scrappy for being my companion, the air of my soul, and asked God to protect her until I meet her again at the Rainbow Bridge in Heaven.

For eight of the twelve and a half years of Scrappy's life, she was a pet therapy dog. Scrappy and I would visit a local children's hospital where the worst of times far outweighed the best of times for the families, doctors, and nurses. Every visit, Scrappy would leave all the patients, their families, the doctors, and the nurses with a smile on their face. Scrappy's job was to help these people feel better about themselves and to give hope to all involved.

Much like any occupation, pet therapy dogs are unique to their field. They go through lengthy training, and must accomplish challenging goals before being permitted to visit. Not all dogs can qualify to be pet therapy dogs, but those that do always leave the places they visit a little happier, and a little better.

A Tail of Love: Life Lessons from Scrappy, a Pet Therapy Dog chronicles many of the life-changing events Scrappy and I encountered together. For all of Scrappy's twelve and half years, she amazed me with her selfless achievements, but it took me many more years than Scrappy's lifespan to understand the true power of those achievements. This book is my attempt to transform her achievements into life lessons for humans.

In my opinion, dogs are the purest form of life. They come to us unbiased, and they only know good. If they learn "bad," it's because a human taught them that. Dogs have much to teach us. We need patience and insight to learn from their integrity and to pass that on to ourselves and others.

I cannot get over Scrappy—she was *that* important to me. I miss her incredibly, to this day. But in her absence, all I can do is reflect, remember, and be thankful for all she taught me.

A five-pound, fuzzy mixture of toy poodle and chihuahua taught me more about life as any human. It is the intent of this book to share with you some of what she taught me. I hope to pass on the life lessons I learned from a pet therapy dog, but most importantly, I hope to share the understanding of why we need to include a little bit of Scrappy's philosophy of love into every day, for the rest of our lives.

Love is a Responsibility

Dogs give unconditional love, and their love is visible. The tail wagging when you come home, the barking of excitement, the wet kisses. The heart of a dog is warm and open for all to see.

Scrappy's love for me was undeniable. Ask anyone who knew Scrappy—her love for me was intentional, absolute, unabashed, and always visible.

Scrappy would greet all of her friends the same way. It would start with a "squeaky" sound she would make. It was not a bark. It was not a whimper. Instead, it was a heartwarming, soothing sound of affection. It was Scrappy's own language. Only she knew what she was saying, but everyone understood what she wanted.

Scrappy would then stand on her hind legs, stretch her front legs as far as she could reach, and continue to make that loving little sound until you reached over and picked her up. After giving them a sweet kiss on the check, she would then ask to be put down so she could come running back to me. Scrappy never ventured far from me, even if we were in the same room together. Some friends could hold Scrappy, but never for long. She was my responsibility, and I was hers.

I believe Scrappy's love was a responsibility. A responsibility is a quality accepted voluntarily, unlike a duty which is a mandated requirement. Through Scrappy's actions, her face, her stares, and her perpetually wagging tail, I know it was a responsibility she accepted willingly.

It is easy for humans to say, "I love you," but how does a dog say it?

Scrappy had beautiful dark eyes that would penetrate deeply into mine, for extended moments. It was not a glance; it was not fleeting. They were long, deep stares of love, appreciation, and gratitude that only Scrappy could deliver. The only picture I have of Scrappy on my desk is of her propped up by the arm of the couch, lying on her back with a blanket around her body. Her head is tilted back, looking at me intently with those amazing eyes. I know what she was saying.

Scrappy's love extended beyond just me, as she was a pet therapy dog for more than eight years. Our primary visitation facility was a children's hospital, which we visited one day a month at first (eventually, our schedule got extended to two days a month). At the hospital, we visited children who suffered everything from illnesses and broken bones to some tragedies you simply could not imagine.

On one occasion, we were asked to go to a floor we rarely visited. We were greeted by a nurse who heard we were in the building. She made a highly unusual request. Would Scrappy please come visit a very young child to try to calm them down? Of course, Scrappy was willing to visit the child—that's what we were here for.

However, I was not permitted to enter the room, as Scrappy and I normally would. The nurse said she would carry Scrappy into the room without me. I had to wait outside the room, out of sight, and down the hallway. And oh, I was asked not to speak.

"We do not want the child to hear your voice," I was told.

This child, the nurse explained, had been sexually assaulted by the father. Upon arrival at the hospital, the child had been understandably inconsolable. The child was surrounded by only female nurses. The fear from the nurses was that the presence of a man—even the sound of my voice—might scare the child, and they may not be able to gain the trust of the child afterward. Any hope of building trust and a protective environment could be lost.

So I gladly put Scrappy into the nurse's arms, told Scrappy to be good, and waited, out of sight, as the two of them entered the child's room.

I could hear the child crying, and the nurse softly say to the child, "Look what I have. Would you like to pet Scrappy?"

As if an angel had been sent from heaven above, the crying began to soften, and eventually disappeared. The only sounds coming from the room were from the other six nurses, saying things like, "how cute," "how sweet," "how soft she is."

Scrappy was that angel sent from above, and she was doing her job well.

Scrappy knew love is a responsibility. She accepted her role as a pet therapy dog and made it her mission to love all she encountered.

I waited for fifteen minutes before Scrappy left the room again with the nurse. With tears in her eyes, the nurse put her finger to her lips to remind me to be quiet. She handed Scrappy back to me, escorted us out the door, and shared with me the miracle Scrappy delivered.

Prior to Scrappy's arrival, no one could calm the understandably confused and afraid young child. Even with seven female nurses surrounding the child, protecting the child, there was no amount of comfort that would soothe the child.

But, the nurse said, as soon as she walked into the room with Scrappy, all the dark clouds for this child cleared. Scrappy became the sun this little child yearned for. The nurse said the child reached out to touch Scrappy's soft hair, put their cheek on Scrappy's side, and finally relaxed. Scrappy sat next to the child while being petted until the child slowly began to close their eyes in comfort. The child was at ease. Thanks to Scrappy, the child began to believe that the nurses had built a safe place and no harm was going to enter that room.

Still with tears in her eyes, the nurse said the other six nurses in that room were crying as well. Scrappy provided the love that not only the child needed but the nurses needed as well.

Love is a responsibility. Even after such a horrific life event, this little child still had the kindness in their heart to love Scrappy, and Scrappy knew to love the child.

This same hospital also specialized in childhood cancer. Under normal circumstances, our visits started in the cancer wing of the hospital. These children needed all the love they could get. They and their families were entering into dark places of life they were simply too young to be entering.

Scrappy's presence was always loudly announced so everyone knew she was coming. Room by room, Scrappy made her way through, greeting and loving everyone she passed. Nurses first then we carefully entered each private patient room. For some of these children it was their first visit. They were nervous, the parents afraid. Scrappy relaxed the fear, broke the tension, and gave anyone that wished a kiss on the nose.

Watching Scrappy display her love to everyone, made me question our sense of love. Often, we say, "I love you," and I am sure it is sincere. But does the frequency of saying "I love you" diminish its meaning? Is our love taken for granted? Is it heartfelt or just rhetoric, something we say out of habit?

Do we treat love like a responsibility?

When I think about love, I cannot help but think about my parents. I reflect on them often, but one situation will stay with me forever.

In early 2019, my father had to enter into hospice for a brief period. On Father's Day, Scrappy, Susie, my mother, and I went to see my father at the hospice facility. Dad was doing well, felt well, and was his usual infectious optimistic self. It was great seeing Dad. I just wish he was not where he was.

After an hour or so of visiting, the doctor entered the room. She asked Dad a few questions about his health, explained a few things to all of us, then surprised us all by saying the only words that truly mattered when you are in hospice: "Do you want to go home?"

Dad started getting out of bed immediately, looking for his shoes, looking for his clothes. Heck yeah, he was ready to go home!

The doctor slowed him down a bit, but needless to say, we started packing his belongings. I took the bags to the car as quickly as I could carry them.

Once we got the "all clear" from the nurse, with the discharge paperwork in hand, I brought the car around and got everyone in. Scrappy was in my lap, Susie in the passenger seat, and Mom and Dad were sitting in the backseat together holding hands, as if they were in high school again.

They were married for sixty-nine-and-three-quarters years (Mom always makes us add the "three quarters"), and they were still holding hands. And they continued to hold hands, even as Dad passed away later that year. That's a real sign of visible love.

Love should not only be seen but felt. When you say, "I love you," let the recipient know it. Say it slowly, say it staring directly into their eyes like Scrappy and my parents did. Say it with emotion and with a sparkle in your eye. Put your hands around their face and say, "I love you."

Love is not just a statement; it is an emotion. Scrappy was an emotional creature. She did not want to disappoint and that is why, I believe, she treated her love as a responsibility. Her love was expressed in so many ways.

Sometimes, she would sit on my arm, exhale, then gently place her head against my chest. In that moment, she knew her love for me was reciprocated. She was protected and secure. She could relax, knowing nothing would happen to her.

Time would stop for both of us at that moment. There was peace. There was calm. As humans, that is what love should be. Love is that emotional state when nothing else matters. Love is silent. Love is accepting. When in love, we have accepted a sobering responsibility to provide security, peace, and warmth to each other.

Be on Call

Have you ever seen a child receive chemotherapy treatments? As a pet therapy team at a children's hospital, Scrappy and I were, unfortunately, witness to countless children who were scheduled to receive their treatment. But there was one specific occasion that will forever be with me.

As we entered the second floor of the children's hospital, Scrappy and I would always stop at the nurses' station first to get the list of the rooms to visit. But there was a greater cause to this first stop: to visit with the nurses. Nurses are the most wonderful people in the world. They are the frontline of care, and they are the ones who must deal with the emotions of the patients and their families. They are underappreciated for their work. They are stressed, bravely holding back their emotions and being the professionals they are trained to be. Scrappy and I would always stop to provide some needed love, a release from their stress, and a brief moment of joy.

On this particular day, Scrappy was greeted with the usual announcement of, "Scrappy is here!" from all the nurses. But this day was different.

We knew something was wrong, because even from the nurses' station, you could hear a child crying uncontrollably. From the opposite corner of the building, a nurse stuck her head around the wall, calmly got our attention, and asked if we could come visit her patient first, before visiting the nurses' desk. There was no objection on our part. As we approached her, she told us her patient was about to receive another round of chemotherapy. This child knew what another round of chemo meant: pain for what would seem like hours.

We entered the room as we always did, with Scrappy perched on my left arm. An early lesson we learned when visiting at the children's hospital was the children could not see Scrappy if she was on the floor walking like most dogs. She was simply too small. To correct the visibility, I started carrying Scrappy on my left forearm. She would place all four of her paws in the palm of my hand, sit on my forearm and rest against my chest. Now, Scrappy was easily visible for even the smallest child.

This was not our first visit with this patient. In fact, we had visited with him multiple times during his years of attendance at the children's hospital, so, he and Scrappy knew each other well.

As we entered his room, he was able to mutter "Scrappy!" through his tears and emotions. Upon seeing Scrappy, the tears continued to flow, but the volume of the crying was reduced significantly.

As the nurse was preparing for his chemo treatment, Scrappy and I sat on the bench in the room with the young patient. Scrappy was between us. It was as if Scrappy completely understood the severity of the situation, as she usually did. She was highly attentive, calm, and ready to do her work. Our patient sat next to Scrappy, put his tiny little hand on Scrappy's back and began petting her as his treatment began.

During chemotherapy treatment, as the IV begins, it creates a chilling effect—"cold" would be more specific. And then it creates heat, burning heat. At this point, our young patient started screaming.

"It's burning, Mommy!"

As much pain as this child was experiencing, his mother was worse. She was helpless to take the pain away from her poor son. The anxiety and need to do something to help her child was intensely showing on her face.

All she could say was, "Focus on Scrappy, baby, she's here to help you."

And she was. Scrappy never flinched. Scrappy was the ballast that stabilized the boat. The tears did not stop, but the child never, ever took his hand off little Scrappy. He petted her nonstop. Finally, the burning slowed, and the chilling effect came back. It was finally over. The tears dried up, and Mom, well, Mom could finally relax too. What seemed like hours of pain ended with a gentle kiss on

Scrappy's head from our patient. Mom hugged us both, thanked us for what we did, and made sure we understood her appreciation.

We had heard this young boy screaming with fear from several hundred feet away, then spent twenty minutes of pure agony while he got his chemo. Scrappy did her work honorably, with dignity and professionalism.

Things were finally calm. Until we saw the patient's nurse.

She was now in tears, and at that moment we knew that Scrappy's job was not complete.

The nurse gently put her hands around Scrappy's tiny face, stared into her eyes, and said, "Thank you." The nurse then turned to me and, with tears in her eyes, said, "Thank you."

The nurse explained that every time she entered her patient's room, the young boy would cry and scream. In his mind, every time she entered his room something bad was about to happen—chemo— and there was nothing she could do about that. She was evil in his mind, and all he knew to do was to scream in terror and cry endlessly when she arrived. There was no comfort for anyone.

Scrappy changed that for the nurse. From that point on, whenever the young boy was about to experience something bad, the young boy's mother would ask the hospital personnel to call us. Everyone knew—Scrappy was on call, and always happy to help. Fortunately, we lived close to the hospital, so when they called, Scrappy responded. No questions asked. Scrappy knew she was on call, and accepted that huge responsibility.

Scrappy understood her role. She was there to offer comfort, to listen, and not to question—just to be there. And sometimes, that is all it takes—just to be there, to be on call, to support our fellow humans.

The future for this little boy was not promising. He spent months in the hospital. We saw him weekly. We met his family, all the way down to cousins. He was often sad or upset, but he was comfortable with Scrappy and Scrappy was comfortable with him.

During one visit, he was strong and feeling great, and he decided he wanted to take Scrappy for a walk.

As innocent as it sounds, the magnitude of walking with Scrappy was enormous. Scrappy was a leader, she was not a follower. She did not adhere to traditional dog-walking obedience protocol. With me, she was always out front, leading the walk—she was not walking by my side, as protocol would dictate. As a lead dog, Scrappy would pull me on our walks to the point of mildly choking herself.

I put the leash in his tiny hand, worried that she would pull him along impatiently, like she did me. Surprisingly, Scrappy waited patiently. The young boy took my hand, and we walked the hallways of the hospital. He was proud, he was smiling, and he was talking constantly.

On this day, Scrappy was patient. She walked side by side with the child, never rushing the walk. It was as if she knew the boy's limited strength. It was a great day for everyone.

Several months later, I saw a billboard with the boy's face on it. The billboard had a simple message: "PRAY." Anyone who saw this billboard understood the message. This boy was a champion. He fought hard, but unfortunately, time and disease were still fighting... and they had the upper hand.

I watched for any news about the child, and before long I sadly learned that the fight was over. A service was being held at a local church. The public was invited to attend and be received by the family. Scrappy and I arrived at the church to join a line of well-wishers over a hundred yards long.

As usual, Scrappy sat on my left forearm. As we waited in line, friends of the family would exit the church, passing by us. Those who knew Scrappy from our hospital visits would stop in amazement at our presence, softly pet Scrappy's head, and comment on how wonderful it was that Scrappy was in attendance.

Without fail, Scrappy's great deeds at the hospital were always mentioned. It was heartwarming for me to hear those acknowledgements and the impact Scrappy had on this boy's life as well as on the lives of his family.

As we entered the sanctuary, I could see the family greeting everyone in line. Mom was at the front of the line, followed by Dad, then aunts and uncles. Mom's attention was singularly focused, never wavering to see who was next in line. Each person had 100 percent of her attention as she took her time to personally thank them for coming by.

I could see the pride in her face. She and her son fought this battle together. From our time together at the hospital, I knew she was realistic and understood the severity of her son's condition, but she was always hopeful. It was obvious she was heartbroken but the pride of being this boy's mother was more powerful than her heartbreak. Her face had a glow that only a proud mother could have.

We were next. I knew she would not know *my* name, but that was not the point. She knew Scrappy, and she knew me as Scrappy's dad. Perfect.

Upon seeing Scrappy, her mouth opened in amazement. She called out Scrappy's name, her hands reached out to Scrappy, and the tears began to flow. The memories of her son with Scrappy immediately warmed her heart with joy, mixed with a little pain as well. Her son rarely ever had a great day, but when Scrappy visited, that time together was always precious. His mother's slow tears were a reminder of the few joyous days of this child's life.

Mom called out Scrappy's name loud enough to cause the receiving line to stop. The family looked up, and then, as if Scrappy were a magnet, the entire family surrounded Scrappy and me in a circle and praised Scrappy with hugs, kisses, and gentle caressing. Scrappy was that important to them. She had impacted this entire family in a way that was difficult to explain. It was powerful. It was moving.

Scrappy was just doing what Scrappy always did. She was compassionate, she was patient, and she was calm. But most importantly, Scrappy was there when necessary. Even though this young boy's life was spent mostly in pain, Scrappy's presence eliminated that pain, put a smile on his face, and warmed his heart.

And at this moment, at this time in their lives, Scrappy did it again for this boy's family. The pain of losing their child was temporarily removed by seeing Scrappy, by petting her soft body, and by remembering the powerful comfort Scrappy brought to their son.

We should all be "on call" for those we love. We have a responsibility to each other. People need each other. Sometimes we need to reach out to someone special, someone we trust. Don't be afraid to reach out to those you love for help, and if someone needs to reach out to you, be on call for them. Be available, and be proactive in making sure those you love are safe. We never know the severity of the situation, but we should never back down from the responsibility. It is *that* important.

Lick the Bowl

Pleasure can come in many forms, but rarely is such pleasure witnessed as when a dog licks the bowl after eating. Licking the bowl, for a dog, is a sign of immense pleasure. Not only was the food exceptional—and so were, perhaps, some treats that were included—but there is also a desire for more. Licking the bowl means that what just happened was great, but I know there is more pleasure to come and that it will be even better the next time.

Scrappy was a funny little eater. Her food was out and available 24/7, yet she would rarely eat until she saw me finish eating. See, I would usually give Scrappy a little bit of what I ate and place it on top of her food.

Scrappy was smart, very smart. There were signs she could detect of the impending, licking-the-bowl moment. Scrappy would wait for the sound of a utensil hitting the plate. That was the clue. In Scrappy's mind, the sound of a utensil hitting a nearly clean plate meant "Dad is almost through eating and now it is my time." You could see those thoughts running through her mind. She would sit up, stare at me with those beautiful eyes, and patiently, very patiently, wait for the second sign.

When it was time, I would look at little Scrappy and say, "Are you ready?" Sign Number Two. She would start spinning around in circles with joy, as if she were doing a dance. Then she'd run to her bowl, already full of kibble, and wait for me to gently place an amount of food that would barely cover my thumbnail on top of her food.

Finally, I would say, "Okay," and she would start eating what I placed on her food first. Then Scrappy would go through her own methodology of eating.

She would not gobble her food down. Scrappy was a delicate eater. Instead, she would take several pieces of kibble out of the bowl, place them on the floor next to the bowl, and then gracefully eat one at a time. She never rushed—she savored. She was licking the bowl in her own way.

As dainty as Scrappy was at eating, she had another very unusual routine after every meal. After each meal, I would hold Scrappy on my forearm. Scrappy would then begin to clean her face. If you did not know better, you may think Scrappy was more cat than dog because of how she cleaned her face. Scrappy would lift her right paw to her mouth, lick the bottom of the paw, and then rub that paw down the right side of her face several times, then the left. The process was all so gentle.

But that is where the delicate, cat-like part of the process ended. Either during or shortly after the face cleaning, Scrappy would return to her dog ways and belch like a fat old man.

A sign of pleasure, I guess. She would belch after every meal. And it was not a lady-like belch. No, it was straight from the gut—loud, prolonged, smelly, but with dignity, as if to assure the chef it was a great meal. Licking the bowl never had greater meaning.

Scrappy discovered her happiness early. Every Sunday, we would go walking through a national park in upstate New York—well, *I* walked. Scrappy would sprint. She would sprint a distance, stop, turn around, and wait for me to catch up. She would never get out of my view.

Occasionally, Scrappy would get just off the trail and wander through the tall grass. I could see her jumping forward through the grass, with her head up, and her legs perched under her, preparing for the impact of the ground to be absorbed. At one point, a couple walked by as Scrappy was leaping through the air and said, "Is that a dog or a kangaroo?"

Scrappy was licking the bowl.

Another way Scrappy licked the bowl was when she discovered her echo. Scrappy would only bark on a few occasions, and she rarely barked inside the house. If she barked inside the house, it was because we would have company over and the guest had not petted her yet. She would stand on her hind legs with her front paws on your leg and bark to get your attention so you were reminded that you had not touched her yet. Once you did, all was right with the world—she was licking the bowl again.

But Scrappy could bark when outside. She knew it, and she loved it. But when she discovered her echo, barking took on a new meaning and purpose. She would intentionally go between our house and the neighbor's house, bark, pause, and relish in the echo she would hear. It was like "buy one, get one free" for Scrappy.

The same was true when we would go to the park, surrounded by trees and mountains. Barking there was the best, because the echoes would multiply. One bark produced multiple barks—this phenomenon was exceptional to Scrappy.

Licking the bowl for Scrappy was easy. It required no effort on her part, because the happiest place for Scrappy was anywhere with me. The same was true for me. We never wanted to be separated. Wherever I was, was where Scrappy wanted to be. And wherever Scrappy was, was where I wanted to be.

It was rare not to see us together. If we visited friends, Scrappy was always welcomed. All our friends kept a personalized water bowl available for her.

We would also drive around town together. Scrappy would be in my lap, and when we came to a stop, she would pop up to look out the window. Invariably, if someone was stopped next to us, they would peer over, smile, or wave to get Scrappy's attention.

Airports were always interesting places for Scrappy. Before security got so tight at airports, Scrappy would be on her leash and we would walk from gate to gate. The looks we'd get from our fellow passengers were just outstanding. Scrappy did not just walk. She had a prance about her. She was proud, excited to see everyone. She got everyone's attention. Once at the gate, Scrappy would sit in my lap and watch everyone pass by. Very often, passers by would ask if it would be OK to take a picture. She was just that cute.

We met some really interesting people in airports. For instance, we were once waiting to go home to upstate New York from San Antonio, TX. While we were sitting at the gate a gentleman came and sat next to us. While admiring Scrappy, he pulled out his pictures of his dog and spoke about how anxious he was to get home to see him. We came to find out that this gentleman was flying back to New York as well. He was on an earlier flight than us, but then he would continue his travels to Lake Placid, New York.

Lake Placid was exactly a two-hour drive from where Scrappy and I lived in New York. I knew this because I visited Lake Placid regularly for the excellent fly fishing and cycling opportunities. Lake Placid is one of my most favorite places in the world.

Lake Placid had also been the host site for two Winter Olympics. As this gentleman and I continued to talk, he told me he immigrated to Lake Placid from the then Soviet Union to be a coach for the United States Olympic Bobsled and Luge Team. Being a huge Olympics fan, I was very interested, and we continued to talk until he boarded the plane. He extended an invitation for me to come to Lake Placid, and said he would arrange a tour of the United

States Olympic Training Facility, under one condition...I had to bring Scrappy!

It is difficult for me to explain the relationship Scrappy and I had. It was a natural friendship, but at the same time, it was the type of relationship most humans do not share or experience. Scrappy only had a couple requirements for me: safety and love. That's all. Everything else was just part of the package. No further expectations. No additional needs. Our relationship was comfortable, without stress. It was one in which we respected one another. One in which just being together was a way of licking the bowl, in and of itself.

It seems odd to compare my relationship with Scrappy in humanistic terms, but that was just the way it was. The closest human comparison is with my best friend. We do not see each other nearly as much as we would like to, but when we do get together, it feels natural. We talk to get caught up on our families and things going on in our lives, but honestly, language is not necessary. We are comfortable in each other's presence without having to expect anything in return.

Scrappy and I were that way. As unnatural as this kind of connection may seem to humans, it was completely natural for Scrappy and me. Scrappy was the happiest when she was with me, and I was the happiest with Scrappy.

Without Scrappy, I feel lost. It is not natural for me to be without her. It is not natural for me to travel without her. Nothing seems right. I struggle at times to find my happiness. I am surrounded by friends, and I am surrounded by love, yet, the challenge to live without Scrappy in my life is hard. It hurts.

Licking the bowl requires us to be happy. That seems obvious, but happiness is not always that easy. We have different components of our lives that impact us more than others. Happiness is sometimes being in silence. Sometimes it is simply holding hands like my parents in the backseat of the car, while other times it is screaming with a thousand of your closest friends at that winning score.

Regardless of your happiness, it still must be discovered. Dogs never really know if what they are going to eat is that exceptional or not. But frankly, it does not always matter. Dogs have the ability to accept without condition what they receive, and celebrate it joyfully regardless. That unconditional love makes dogs so special.

Dogs lick the bowl because they are happy—they hunger for more. As humans, we need to follow their lead: lick the bowl, then go back for more. Happiness is essential for all beings. It can come in different forms—whether physical or emotional, but happiness just does not happen. It must be sought for, it must be discovered. And when discovered, it must be celebrated. We have to discover our happiness in order to lick the bowl.

Scrappy taught me happiness is a choice. It is an acceptance of our desire to reach a higher level of life—it is our ability to lick the bowl. It has taken me close to two years for me to lick the bowl. It has been a challenge. Now, memories turn most of my tears to smiles. My heart warms and is light with life. I can now lick the bowl.

Take Time to Bring your Emotions to Tears

Jim Valvano, the former head men's basketball coach at North Carolina State University, stated in his infamous March 3, 1993, ESPN ESPY Awards speech, "When people say to me, 'How do you get through life or each day?', it's the same thing. To me, there are three things we should all do every day. We should do this every day of our lives. Number one is to laugh. You should laugh every day. Number two is to think. You should spend time in thought. Number three is you should have your emotions moved to tears, could be happiness or joy."[1]

1 https://www.v.org/about/remembering-jim/espy-awards-speech/

Those are powerful words, especially when you are dying of cancer as Jim Valvano was at the time of his speech. The first two are easy. It is easy to laugh, and it is easy to think every day. We do both without much thought or effort.

But to bring your emotions to tears takes strength. To cry requires a release of your inner strength and humility, to share what is perceived to be a weakness.

However, I feel crying is a strength. It is nothing to be ashamed of.

When you are brought to tears, you admit you care. You admit you have reached a level of such singular significance that your passion must come rolling down your face for all to see. It takes personal strength to show that level of emotion, but it also shows your commitment.

The first time my emotions were brought to tears with Scrappy was when she was eight years old. Scrappy had just been diagnosed with cancer. The "C" word. The six-letter, four-letter word no one ever wants to hear had become a part of my life for the very first time.

We never had to deal with cancer in our immediate family. We had always visited children who had cancer, and we knew how to comfort and to provide a distraction, but now cancer was in our family. I was afraid, and I felt helpless.

It happened so quickly. Scrappy seemed fine. Her routine was the same. There was no pain, no evidence of anything being wrong. We were going away to the mountains for a long weekend. The car was packed, we were ready to go. Then all of a sudden, Scrappy became sluggish. She was moving, but not as freely as normal. Something was not right, but there was no visible sign to detect.

We drove an hour to our destination. Scrappy was not in my lap during the drive which was an immediate sign something was not right with her. Instead she layed in her bed for most of the trip. When we arrived, I held Scrappy to let her out of the car so she could do her business. And there it was. A lump. A very large lump protruding from her belly that had not been there an hour ago. Scrappy could not relieve herself, and her pain was now obvious.

I put Scrappy back on her bed and placed the bed in my lap. We were going home. I called her veterinarian, explained the situation, and met her at her hospital. A quick examination confirmed it was a tumor. It was serious. Scrappy would have surgery the very next morning, and she had to stay the night at the hospital.

We had never been separated overnight like this. My fears were getting worse, but I was hopeful her condition would improve after surgery.

I gave Scrappy a goodnight kiss on the head, then held her as long as I could before the doctor took her away. The tears were gushing down my face. I was scared. I had to wait for the doctor to explain to me what was about to happen. She explained they would examine the tumor, remove it, and remove a little extra tissue for margin. The surgery would take place first thing in the morning, and she would call as soon as it was over.

It felt like it took a week for the next morning to arrive. I had not slept. I had not eaten. I have never felt so helpless and afraid, and I was beginning to understand how the parents Scrappy and I visited each week felt when they were told "Your child has cancer." It was absolutely horrible.

The call finally came that the surgery went well; Scrappy was in recovery and doing fine. I was permitted to visit Scrappy for just a moment that evening. The doctor walked me in and showed me the crate where Scrappy was in recovery. I called her name and her eyes, covered in glaze, looked my way. A look of joy came over her face when she saw me.

"Hey, baby girl," I said. She struggled to stand and walk toward me. She was attempting to talk with me, but her squeaky little voice was weak. I reached in, touched her, and said, "Lay down. You need to rest." And she did. I rubbed her head, told her "I love you," then let her get the necessary recovery rest she needed.

A couple days later, Scrappy was able to come home, and I cried again. I was relieved everything went well. I was able to breathe again. I was able to take care of my baby girl. I was able to hold her in my arms.

Cancer free! Scrappy was free of the disease that had so quickly wrested her.

Scrappy recovered perfectly from cancer. We now had a story to tell all the children we visited in similar situations.

"Scrappy had cancer just like you. She did everything her doctors told her and look at her now. And your doctors are going to take care of you just like Scrappy's doctor took care of her. It's going to be okay."

I do think the story helped the children. They began to see in Scrappy that they could get better, knowing Scrappy got better. Confidence is critical in times of fear. Scrappy was able to show confidence when fear of the unknown was at the highest levels possible.

Since Scrappy's passing, I have brought my emotions to tears nearly every day—some more than others. I feel a loss that cannot be replaced in this physical world, and I am at a loss as to what to do without her. When anyone mentions Scrappy's name, my eyes water, my throat tightens, and my heart saddens. Scrappy meant that much to me. She was more than a pet. Scrappy was the air of my soul.

For me, my tears for Scrappy come from numerous situations. Some are more complicated than others. For instance, one particular dog food TV commercial makes me tear up every single time I see it. Ironically, it's not tears of sadness. Instead, it is tears of pride.

The first scene is of a beautiful little girl lying in a hospital bed with her mother by her side. Scrappy and I saw this scene countless times at the children's hospital. It's a sad moment to see a child in a hospital bed. You feel helpless. But to see a mother next to their child in a hospital bed is the worst. You can feel their fear and uncertainty, and all you want to do is provide some kind of relief. To make it all better.

As the commercial develops, the little girl extends her left arm down the length of the bed and says to a nurse entering her room, "more treatment" as if she was anticipating being poked with another needle.

My heart breaks with every word and emotion coming from this little girl. Again, Scrappy and I saw this more times than anyone should ever have to experience.

The scene changes from our little patient to a nurse standing in the doorway of her cold, isolated hospital room. The nurse is the hero, as they always are. She has come to the rescue of the child.

The nurse explains, "We're going to try something new this time."

Then enters a pet therapy dog.

As it always was when Scrappy entered a room, the face of the little girl changes from despair to pure joy. She says, "Ahhh!" and the most beautiful smile you would ever see comes to her face. She gently rolls her body to the left side of her bed as a wonderful pet therapy dog with a red bandana around its neck comes to the side of the bed and greets the little girl, gently placing its head on the side of the bed. The dog is in perfect view for the little girl to touch.

This unassuming dog food commercial makes me cry every time. It takes me back to a friendly place. A place where Scrappy made everyone in any room she entered happy. A place where Scrappy, like the dog in the commercial, made fear disappear. It's a beautiful sight and a beautiful memory. I miss those moments terribly.

This commercial does for me what Jim Valvano was telling everyone in the world that was watching him that day—it makes me "take time." These two simple words deliver the most impactful message. Take time to slow down. Take time to reflect. Take time to laugh.

Take time to think. Take time to bring your emotions to tears. If we do not take time, we can not accomplish any of those things.

In our non-stop world, we must force ourselves to take time. It is critical for us to pause occasionally, to put down all the technology and escape our immediate realities so we can enter a place of serenity.

I am reminded of a *Seinfeld* episode where one of the characters becomes so anxious, so tense, that he screams, "Serenity now! Serenity now!" This comedic relief illustrates a critical component to our lives that we too often ignore. Serenity provides us all the opportunities to reflect. Serenity provides us opportunities to reach the level of calm necessary to continue our movements of life.

Taking time sounds so simple—and it can be. But it can also be difficult. We are too busy nowadays. We have too many demands on us. Taking time can be difficult, but not taking time can cause dangerous levels of anxiety.

So take time to bring your emotions to tears. Strength will be the reward.

Tears do not have to come from a place of sadness. Tears can also come from a sense of pride.

Scrappy makes me very proud. I was proud of her every time we visited the children's hospital. She would work so hard. She would accomplish so much. That pet therapy dog in the commercial is a realistic representation of what Scrappy would accomplish on her visits. Scrappy lived that commercial hundreds of times during her lifetime.

Do not be afraid to allow your emotions to come to tears. My tears are often the result of pride.

For instance, I am proud to be the son of my parents. My parents taught me, showed me, and provided for me the foundation of my life and purpose. That makes me emotional. Since my father's passing, I cry a little more when I think of all they did for me.

I think about my best friend from college and his accomplishments. To know how immature we were in college, seeing where he is today makes me proud. He is married and is raising two incredible children. He decided to become a triathlete, overcame brain cancer, and excels professionally—all of that makes me emotional. Even though I am not directly in his life, I am a part of his life as his friend. How proud I am of my friend.

Success is an emotion that brings me to tears. It does not have to be my success—in fact, it is just the opposite. Success in *others* is what brings my emotions to tears. Too often, people want to destroy, discredit, or humiliate others. Why do we tolerate such behavior? My emotions are not brought to tears when this happens. Success should be celebrated; seeing other people succeed should bring our emotions to tears.

Scrappy does that for me. It is not just her loss that brings my emotions to tears. It is what she did with her life. She made the most of it, she did all that was asked of her, and she made a difference. She made people smile, laugh, and feel better about the day.

I mentioned earlier that people often knew Scrappy's name, but no one knew mine. I was always only known as Scrappy's dad. I proudly accepted that name. That is a name that brings my emotions to tears.

Make a difference with your life. Make it impactful on others. When done, I promise you, you will be able to bring your emotions to tears. Those tears will make you stronger for the rest of your life.

Be More than a Pet

Pets, to me, are the greatest invention known to man. Where else can we go to feel immediate, responsive, and visible love? Where else can we go to have a purpose? Where else can we go to know that we are appreciated?

Pets provide all of those voluntarily. It comes with the territory. But most pets stay at home. Unfortunately, a pet's territory can be restricted and limited, but the power of pets is truly released when their exposure to the world is opened.

Scrappy was an explorer. She was never hesitant to venture beyond her immediate territory, as long as I remained in view. We traveled together, all over the country, by car, by train, and by plane. She loved it. She was always ready for the next adventure.

I was fortunate to have built my business such that travel was sometimes necessary. Working with professional associations provided me with an extremely large base of potential new clients, but it also provided me the opportunity to speak publicly about our industry and how our services could be of benefit to each member.

As is common with any convention, vendors, like me, could set up a table with literature and speak with attendees walking by. However, anyone in sales knows that you must work on the friendly side of business before you can get to the business side of business. If you have ever worked at professional conventions, you know you must have a catch, something that is going to draw people to your booth so that you can engage in conversation.

I had the catch. I had the eye-grabber. I had Scrappy!

Scrappy was the best salesperson I ever had—she was a natural. She could draw a crowd without ever saying a word. Scrappy had a personality everyone wanted to be a part of. She would sit on top of the table at our booth and view the scene. If she saw movement, she would start her signature sales call.

First, Scrappy would make eye contact. As soon as someone noticed her—something they had *never* seen at a professional conference before—they would come over.

Second, as soon as Scrappy saw someone venture our way, she would wag her tail and begin to make her squeaky sounds of happiness.

Scrappy was trained not to bark inside—outside was a different story, but when Scrappy was inside, she would make irresistible heartwarming sounds of love no one could resist. Even the most stern professional could not show disdain toward Scrappy. Everyone would eventually hear about the dog at their conference and make their way over to us.

Step three was standing to greet all attendees. Scrappy made eye contact, got their attention, and soon we saw them come our way. Now it was time to show gratitude and appreciation for their efforts. She would stand, continue to wag her tail, and squeak just a little. As soon as they touched her, the squeaking ended. Now it was up to me to close the deal.

Together, Scrappy and I made the perfect sales team. She was the bait, and I was the closer. We worked magic together.

I would like to believe that a bit of Scrappy's gift was due to her ability to see the world beyond our yard. She was not afraid to experience something new. It allowed her to learn. It allowed her to understand that not everyone is the same—we are all different. She was willing and able to accept differences, willing to accept compromises, and willing to adjust accordingly. Her willingness to accept differences without challenge should teach us how we humans should work together.

Scrappy saw the airport employees as her friends, even when the TSA had to swipe their wand over her body to make sure she was not concealing anything. As funny as it was to see a metal detector wand go over her tiny little body, Scrappy was fine with it. Scrappy did not understand, but she did not need to understand. She accepted the procedure for what it was—a process that simply had to be performed. So why fight it? It did not hurt anyone. Patience and understanding were important life principles Scrappy could teach to anyone.

Scrappy allowed the hotel personnel to hold her during check-in. I would place her on top of the counter for all to see, and the employees would all come over to check out the new little soul. Scrappy was unique. Scrappy was comfortable in these new environments, as long as I was there. Scrappy learned from each of these experiences, which made her pet therapy skills even stronger.

Of all the traveling Scrappy and I did, I believe her favorite trips were on trains. Occasionally I would travel into New York City on a commuter train. Commuter trains can be a blessing and a curse for travelers. The blessing is that you will, eventually, get to your destination. The curse is that commuter trains are not the express route. You stop at all the little towns along the way so more passengers can board.

Scrappy loved the train though. She would sit on the inside seat, watching all of the passengers get on and off. It was as if Scrappy was at a tennis match, watching the passengers to the left, then right, then left, then right, until everyone was seated. Then she would wait for the next stop and repeat. I had a great time watching Scrappy watch everyone, and then watching everyone on the train watch Scrappy. It made the long ride go by much faster.

Scrappy had a natural curiosity, a willingness to explore, which I wanted to develop as much as possible. Her natural acceptance is why she was always much more than a pet. Scrappy was family, and it extended beyond my immediate family.

I was a member of a local Rotary Club that met for breakfast on Thursday mornings. Often, Scrappy would have pet therapy immediately after our meetings. With the country club's permission, Scrappy would attend our Rotary meetings with me.

I would place Scrappy in a chair where she would greet everyone. Just as she did at conventions, Scrappy would stand, wag her tail, and squeak until you acknowledged her by name or petted her. Rarely did she allow anyone to pass without some form of acknowledgement.

Scrappy would then disappear into my lap as we began our meetings. At the conclusion, she would wake invigorated, ready to go to work at the children's hospital.

She was the subject of one of our Rotary lectures, sharing our experiences as a pet therapy dog to our members. When appropriate, Scrappy would attend club service events. She was even included in our club photos. We jokingly suggested that Scrappy was an unofficial, honorary member of our club. In reality, her attendance surpassed some of our actual members. Scrappy would have been a tremendous member of Rotary International. She certainly satisfied the motto: "Service Above Self."

Scrappy's desire to explore extended to food as well—however, if it was green, Scrappy would tend to shy away from it. Much like kids, green vegetables were unacceptable. Carrots were OK though.

As long as I was with her, Scrappy was comfortable putting herself in situations where it was OK for her to learn, to experience, and to mature. These experiences made her a better pet therapy dog.

As humans, we need to have the same desire to explore as Scrappy. Life does not have to stop outside our walls of comfort. Humans develop by experiencing. Humans develop by appreciating. Humans develop by exploring. Get out, appreciate, and explore. It will make us better humans.

Fortunately, we all have the tools now to do that. It is not necessary to have a lot of money. It is not necessary to board a plane. We can walk, ride, or surf the net to discover new opportunities and new worlds. If we do not, it is our fault. There is so much beauty in the world that needs to be explored. It is the simple pleasures in life that can give us so much. It can ease our mind. It can give us a yearning for the next corner. It will cause us to be like Scrappy on the train—always looking left, right, left, right for the next point of joy.

Scrappy was never just a pet. She took advantage of our ability to experience life at so many different levels. We grew together as friends from these experiences. She was a part of many families, but most importantly, she was my family.

Wag Your Tail

Dogs wag their tails to show happiness, joy, love, and appreciation.

But have you ever noticed that some dogs wag their tails a little more than others? In fact, some dogs wag their tails so vigorously it causes their entire body to wiggle. That kind of vigor must be pure happiness. What a great feeling that must be. It simply could not get any better. It probably brings a smile to your face as you read this, because we have all seen dogs do this.

This kind of happiness must involve either a special person or a special place. It can not be experienced alone.

Who is that special person that causes you to wiggle all over when you see them? Are you that person for someone else? Wouldn't it be one of your greatest life achievements if you knew you caused such a happy reaction in someone that they wiggled uncontrollably like a dog?

Scrappy was that special for so many children at the hospital. Even though a hospital is a place to heal and get better, it can be a very lonely place. Your day is spent in bed, normally with little to do other than watch TV. It is, of course, interrupted throughout the day by nurses, doctors, and the occasional visitor. But for a young child unable to comprehend the complexity of beeping devices, wires and tubes attached to your body, hospitals are not the fun parks children would prefer to attend.

But then enters Scrappy. Scrappy was there for one reason and one reason only—to allow that child the opportunity to forget about the wires and tubes and all the sounds in their room. Scrappy was there to offer comfort, to be a release of fear for the children, and to create a diversion. And she did her job perfectly.

Most every time Scrappy would enter a room, the reaction would be the same. Eyes would get a little larger, mouths would open a little wider. The most used word when a child saw Scrappy was "Aahhhh!" Scrappy had the ability to make these children wag their tail with excitement. If a child was lying down in bed when Scrappy entered, they would scurry as quickly as possible to sit up. These children would reach out to hold Scrappy or to pet her. Their reaction was much like the excitement a dog shows when they see their favorite human.

Even though they had never met Scrappy, they seemed to know that dogs can cure all. They knew this was a special moment the hospital provided them, and they knew nothing else mattered at this moment. This little visitor entering their room was special. This little visitor was going to make them feel joy and happiness for the first time in a long time. This little visitor was going to give them all the love she could muster. And for the entire time of the visit, this child, in their own way, was going to wag their tail as hard as they could until the visit was over. For the little child, the memory of that very short visit would never, ever go away.

The power of a pet therapy dog is amazing. To be able to release such emotion from a child is only understandable by experience.

Scrappy got excited about the visits, too. She always recognized the entrance to the children's hospital and would start her "squeaking" as soon as we entered the property. The squeaking would continue while we parked, got out of the car, and until we got inside the children's hospital. As a pet therapy dog, it is critical that the animals be calm and relaxed while they visit with the children. Because of that, we would arrive at the hospital fifteen minutes in advance just to give Scrappy some time to calm down before we started our visitation routine.

"Wagging your tail" for Scrappy was her way of expressing excitement of what's to come. Scrappy did not just walk. She had a prance about her. She was proud, excited to see everyone. She got everyone's attention. For Scrappy, "wagging your tail" was sprinting to the front door of the hospital, greeting the receptionist, watching people go in and out of the hospital entrance door, and then finally being welcomed by our Child Life Specialist to begin our rounds. It was part of the process for Scrappy. She absolutely loved this hospital. Scrappy knew she was a star, but carried on about her work as a true professional. She was humble in the love she received but generous in the love she gave.

There was always a child that needed Scrappy—some more than others. She would lay next to them in bed or simply stay on my left forearm as the children would pet her. Scrappy's calm demeanor was comforting, even for those children who did not necessarily like dogs. Countless times, Scrappy would warm the hearts of those who were reluctant to pet her. Every time, when they did pet Scrappy, you could see the happiness in their eyes, their smiles, or their soft laughs—they were beginning to wag their tails. The greatest thank you we could ever get was the request to come back—Scrappy never failed to return.

However, most visits with the children were brief. After all, when you have three floors to visit in a single day, you must keep moving forward. In addition, for the benefit of the dog, most pet therapy organizations suggest that the total visiting time be limited to no more than one hour to prevent emotional exhaustion. Sometimes that was possible, other times impossible. The need was just too great.

Fortunately, Scrappy was willing to extend her visits when necessary. But it did take a toll on Scrappy over the years. In the car, she would fall into my lap a little faster, a little harder. She would rest longer. She was slower to respond to the fun activities she enjoyed. In reality, Scrappy was just getting older.

Scrappy lived to be twelve and a half years of age. During that time, Scrappy taught me a lot about "wagging your tail" that continues to live with me today.

She taught me that friends are the most likely element of life to make your tail wag with happiness. Friends make a person's life whole. Friends keep us motivated. Friends keep us human. Without friends, life is empty and lonely.

I mentioned before that hospitals, for all the good they do, can be very isolating—particularly for children. Hospitals are there to protect us, but in doing so they may, therefore, prevent us from having physical social contact with friends. Hospitals are essential, but can also be a necessary evil at times.

This is why pet therapy visits are so important. Scrappy did not know these children. She was there to comfort them, to make them happy, to make them feel like they had a friend, even if they may never see each other again.

Some of these children would go home and recover from whatever reason they were in the hospital. Hopefully, we would never see them again. They would go on to live healthy, normal lives. However, others would not be so fortunate.

Much like how Scrappy taught me that love is a responsibility, so is friendship. Friends do not have to come in a great quantity, but the best friends come in good quality. We may be happy to see a thousand people, but only a few will we call our friends. These are the ones we love to see. These are the ones we love. These few are the ones who make us wag our tail.

Scrappy taught me we greet our friends differently from other people. With some we may fist bump. With some, we just shake hands. But with our true friends, we hug them a little longer, the kiss on their cheek is a little softer. All are acceptable forms of greeting someone; they simply show a different level of relationship we have with each other and should not be interpreted as anything else.

There may be times in our lives when we underestimate our own personal value. But Scrappy taught me that no matter how we may view our personal significance, there is always someone who sees value in ourselves. They need us. They need our comfort. We should be that friend when necessary.

If any of those children felt isolated, underappreciated, Scrappy removed all of those fears. That child had value to Scrappy, and Scrappy responded by making them feel like they were the most important person in the room.

"Wagging your tail" requires effort. It's hard work. As Scrappy taught me, we can not be friends with everyone; it's simply impossible. People are all different. There are characteristics about all of us that we prefer more than others. It's only natural that we gravitate to those characteristics in people we have in common.

Scrappy demonstrated to me, no matter what our life differences may be, no matter what our uncommon life histories may be, or whether we will ever see one another again, we can always be friendly toward each other.

What do you do when you see that very special person in your life? You smile. Smiling for humans is the equivalent of a dog wagging its tail. Smiling offers the very first indication of love, of appreciation. Anatomically, smiles are easier to achieve than frowns. If dogs can easily wag their tails at the first opportunity to greet someone, we certainly can do the same by smiling a lot more.

As much love as Scrappy provided, I will always remember how graciously she accepted love. Scrappy never questioned why she received the love she got. She was there to give love. Yet, Scrappy seemed to understand reciprocation. She gave love to hundreds of children and she received love from hundreds of children. Regardless of who gave Scrappy love, she accepted the kindness graciously. Love is as important to give as it is to receive.

I believe humans are attracted to dogs so much because they are like us in many ways. Dogs want love. Dogs want security. Dogs want food. We are no different in that respect. However, unlike humans, dogs do not question. Dogs only accept graciously and give back in the same manner. We humans need to learn to do the same. Accept your gifts of love in the same manner as you give your gifts of love—unconditionally, without further expectations or explanations.

Let someone know you appreciate them by wagging your tail. It could be an extended hug or a soft kiss, holding hands or throwing an arm across their shoulder. No matter the sign, make sure you wag your tail. It will always cause someone else to wag their tail in return.

Find the Right Spot

Have you ever petted your dog in such a place or manner that causes them to stop in their tracks? If so, you found *just the right spot*. That right spot causes a complete distraction from everything going on in the world. That right spot creates an overwhelming sense of pleasure so intense that nothing else matters. Some dogs can be rubbed in just the right spot to cause their leg to flex and start kicking. It may be the object of humor for humans, but for the dog, it is pure heaven. It feels so good, it is so relaxing, and it is just the right spot.

The right spot can be a physical location or an emotional state of mind that transforms our mental status. Scrappy had two "right spots."

Scrappy was known in our area for many things, but the one everyone will remember and recognize was how we traveled. Scrappy only weighed five pounds, and she walked close to the ground. As long as there were no other people in the area, Scrappy was very comfortable being like a normal dog—she walked on all four paws. But, when in traffic with other humans, I would pick Scrappy up and carry her. This is not unusual for small dogs; most owners gladly hold their dogs. But Scrappy had her own way of being carried. She would sit on my left forearm, place all four paws in the palm of my hand, and lean back, resting her back against my bicep with her rear end nestled in the angle of my elbow.

Scrappy spent a lot of time sitting this way on my arm, and it served multiple purposes. First, it provided a place of safety. It kept her off the ground and away from human feet that may not see her, because she was so small.

Second, Scrappy was a little dainty. Anything to keep her from getting dirty was appreciated by her. And if she was not dirty, Scrappy would not have to take a bath. Scrappy hated baths. She did not like water, she did not like getting wet. If there was the smallest amount of water on the ground, she would jump over it to prevent from having to walk through it. But when it was necessary for a bath, she knew. First the collar would come off and those beautiful little eyes would get larger with concern. She would hear the water run and begrudgingly walk into the bathroom. I would be kneeling by the tub, checking the water temperature, when Scrappy would sadly sit next to me waiting for the misery to begin.

Most importantly about the "right spot" was that it brought Scrappy into the human world. After all, Scrappy was always more human than dog. Sitting on my arm allowed her to see eye to eye with everyone else. It gave her a new perspective that she could not experience by constantly looking up if she was on the ground.

But the right spot was most critical for her work at the children's hospital. During her pet therapy training sessions, dogs and their handlers must pass certain key "safety" issues. For instance, one test involved the trainers placing a hotdog on the floor. The handlers would then have to walk their dog within a few feet of the hotdog. The dog could not make an attempt to grab the hotdog and eat it, or they would fail.

As silly as this may sound, the hotdog test was a very important test. In a hospital environment, the opportunity exists to walk past medication that may have fallen on the ground or some kind of liquid that is not water. The dogs are taught to "leave it" and continue walking by. Fortunately for Scrappy, she was never a "treats-motivated" dog. Her training desire was to learn and not disappoint me. Her reward was being held by me.

At the children's hospital, finding the right spot on my left arm resolved the safety concerns but, most importantly, it put Scrappy eye to eye with the children. We learned early on during our visits that if Scrappy was on the floor like a regular dog, the child would never see Scrappy when we entered their room. They only saw me, a stranger they had no interest in meeting. But if Scrappy was in her right spot, the children could see her and get excited to meet her.

We could enter the room with the child's attention completely focused on Scrappy and nothing else. We could stand next to the bed with Scrappy in her right spot and the children did not have to stretch or struggle to pet her. With Scrappy sitting on my forearm, all four paws in the palm of my hand, her back resting against my bicep and her rear end nestled into the corner of my elbow, Scrappy was in her right spot.

Everyone always thought that this position was funny, and it was. How often do you see a dog sitting on someone's forearm being carried around? I would often joke with the children that Scrappy had four legs, but her favorite mode of transportation was on my left arm. It not only demonstrated the right spot, but it was a way of easing the tension when life is not so favorable. Hospitals have a way of being tense for everyone, not just for the patients, so any simplistic humor was always welcomed.

This position was also important for her *second* right spot. Sitting the way she did on my forearm allowed Scrappy's chest to be exposed, which she always wanted rubbed. Rubbing her chest not only comforted her but it gave her a sense of security. It was her security blanket of sorts. It was Scrappy's other "right spot."

Scrappy was not shy about letting you know that she wanted her chest rubbed. She would raise up on her hind legs and lift her front legs high. As soon as you started rubbing her chest, the front legs would come down. She would sit comfortably, sigh deeply and enjoy the moment. It was as if she had just settled into a freshly drawn hot bath. All the tension in her body dissipated, a sense of peace overcame her, and nothing was going to interrupt this moment.

My left arm also served a valuable purpose for Scrappy when she was tired and needed some rest. Scrappy would crawl into my lap and wait for my left arm to gently wrap around her so she could sleep. Her head would rest in the angle of my elbow and my left hand would hold her comfortably in place. Immediately, the eyes would close, her breathing slowed. Sleep came easily to her.

Scrappy needed lots of time to rest. The duties of a pet therapy dog are strenuous. She would sense the anxiety of the children, and she would absorb that anxiety to remove it from the children and provide them some peace. The anxiety would turn to exhaustion, for Scrappy. Scrappy needed to dispose of this absorbed anxiety so she could find her peace. Nestling in my lap with my left arm wrapped around her provided her the security and peace she deserved. If my arm was not available to her, a blanket in the sunshine would suffice. Much like that warm bath, the exhaustion would dissipate from Scrappy while lying in the sun. After all, rest is an essential aspect of life. Rest would recharge her with emotional energy for the next visit.

Without Scrappy in my life, I needed to find *my* right spot. My heart was in pain. My left arm was empty. What was I to do, to find my right spot? I still do not know if I have quite found it, but I do know where to go to get help.

A day or two after Scrappy's passing, a couple of our friends came over to console Susie and me, hug us, and help in any way they could to make us feel better. They did that without ever knowing just how much better they made me feel.

It wasn't the wine. It wasn't the hugs. It wasn't the memories we spoke about. It was their dog, Jackson, that made me feel better. Jackson and Scrappy were good buddies. Jackson and Scrappy would often go visit each other and play in each other's yards. Jackson had been here before, but something was different. Something was missing, and Jackson sensed it.

Dogs have an amazing ability to sense the abnormal much better than humans. Jackson was aware, alert to the differences of the moment.

We moved outside to the porch with our glasses of wine. I sat in silence while comforting conversation began. Without any commands or prompting, Jackson moved in between Susie and me. He just sat there. He did not move. We both put our hands on Jackson and never stopped petting his back.

I had become that little boy in the hospital getting his chemo treatment. Just like Scrappy was the right medicine for that little boy, Jackson became my pet therapy dog for that moment. As I silently cried, I never took my hand off of Jackson. He was patient with me. He was what I needed, and he came to comfort me.

Jackson still comes to visit me. He comes over frequently. He understands his role for me. With each visit, I am reminded of what he did for me in my moment of need. I put my hands around his head, stare into his eyes, tell him I love him, and gently place a little kiss on his head. Jackson knows love is a responsibility too and Jackson provided me the right spot when I needed it the most.

Finding the right spot is important because it must come from someone or something else—it cannot be duplicated by ourselves. As humans, we need to know we are appreciated and understood. The right spot gives us comfort, but it can also give a feeling of gratitude or reward for doing a job well. The right spot reward motivates us to do it again and again with greater enthusiasm each time. Partners, significant others, spouses, or bosses all need to discover that right spot. It makes everyone feel better. It makes for greater achievements. It makes for better relationships.

When asked what I miss most about Scrappy, this is it. Scrappy always—and I mean always—sat on my left forearm. It was our identity. And I would always rub her chest. I knew it made her feel better, but for me, it was the touch of her soft hair. She would always tilt her head up and stare into my eyes to let me know of her love and appreciation. I would stare back and utter, "I love you too." I miss Scrappy sitting on my left forearm. I miss rubbing her chest. I miss knowing that I found the right spot for little Scrappy, and I miss her finding the right spot for me.

Control the Room

Have you ever been at an event full of people, when suddenly a beautiful woman enters the room? Just like in the movies, all heads turn, a small silence spreads, and people become mesmerized by her presence. All activity in the room stops and does not restart until the woman, somehow, acknowledges everyone staring. She was not announced to the room, but her presence was so strong the room announced her.

That was what it was like when Scrappy entered a room. Admittedly, Scrappy was cute—very cute. But when she entered a room, Scrappy could control the reactions of everyone in the room. No announcement of her presence had to be made. The room acknowledged her and gravitated in her direction, as if to witness her greatness.

Scrappy entered a room in the same fashion each and every time—sitting on my left arm. She never entered a room walking on her own legs—that would not be natural. Scrappy was usually the smallest creature in the room, but she was always the largest in charm.

It was as simple as that. A cute little dog sitting on her owner's left arm (never the right arm), and all attention would turn to Scrappy. Scrappy could control the entire room without ever making a sound. No barking. No wild gyrations of her body. Just her presence. Just her confidence.

This is a lesson all humans should learn. Make your presence known, through your presence alone. Loudness does nothing for me. In fact, I would rather go the opposite direction of a loud person. Give me someone with confidence, an understanding of who they are. That is where I want to go. Scrappy had the same approach. People would automatically gravitate to her, want to touch her, want to speak with her and do all the silly things we do with small dogs. Obligingly, Scrappy would honor their desires with courtesy and dignity.

I love to see the reaction of dogs when their owners dress them up. Just like humans, some dogs relish the idea of getting dolled up. It is part of their personality. I have seen bulldogs wear masculine leather jackets, imitating the toughness of bikers. I have seen dainty little dogs like Scrappy wear princess outfits, showing off their "diva-ness." I think these activities are more fun for the humans than it is the dogs, but it certainly creates a lively environment.

Scrappy really did not care to dress up. She tolerated it. In fact, if we held up a dress we bought at a pet store, she would look at us as if saying, "You've got to be kidding. Not again!" All we had to do was hold it in front of her face and a look of disdain was immediate. Fortunately for us, Scrappy always reluctantly agreed to wear the dress for very special events.

Once, we attended a fundraiser for a local animal shelter. It was a "black tie" event, including for the dogs. Dogs and their humans were dressed to the nines, showing off to everyone as we gathered on the second floor of the event center. Smiles dominated the evening. Laughter was plenty.

Scrappy wore a beautiful pink sundress with white polka-dots. I wore a matching tie with my suit, and Susie wore a formal black dress. Scrappy, of course, stood out from the crowd—because of her pink dress, but also because she entered the room sitting on my left arm, as usual.

It was a wonderful evening altogether, but there were two distinct moments when Scrappy completely controlled the room.

The first was a photo shoot. The organizers arranged to have photos taken of all the participants. Ordinarily, the photographer would take one photo of each couple and their dog and then move on. There were just too many participants for multiple shots. However, for us, the photographer had to take several pictures because Scrappy was doing her magic, controlling the room. Unbeknownst to anyone except the photographer, for the first photograph, Scrappy daintily and politely stuck her tongue out at the camera as the photo was being taken. Susie was in her black formal evening gown, I was in a formal suit, and Scrappy was in a polka-dot pink dress, sticking her tongue out at the camera. *Click.*

Timing is everything, I guess, but was this just timing, or was Scrappy sending a message? Scrappy really did not like dressing up. Was she trying to tell me something? I think the answer is yes. Regardless, it is my favorite picture, and I proudly display it in my office.

The second occasion was during the fundraising event itself. At one point, the organizers wanted to have a fashion show where all the dogs would walk across the catwalk (no pun intended) and show off their outfits. It was a great opportunity to show off all the clothes, have a little bit of fun, and get all the attendees in a donate-more-money kind of mood.

Well, much like a preacher trying to get the back row congregation members to move to the front row, there was an awkward silence in the room when the fashion show was announced. No one was moving toward the stage. Everyone was just looking at each other, waiting for someone else to make the first move.

Finally, Scrappy decided to control the room and get the line started. She was the first dog to cross the catwalk. She immediately came to life as the crowd cheered and cameras flashed. She paraded to the end of the catwalk like a professional model. She proudly stood at the end of the stage, allowed herself to be photographed, then stood on her hind legs like a meerkat looking for something. The crowd laughed and applauded as Scrappy turned in a circle so everyone could see the intricate details of her dress, then off the stage she went. None of her antics were asked of her; I was silent the entire time. Scrappy performed on her own, in her own way, without any encouragement from me.

In the performing arts world and sometimes in business, elite people are often described as having the "it" factor. The "it" factor is a unique quality within someone that is appealing to nearly everyone in the world. It is not anything specific, and can not be explained in a way that makes sense. It is not obtainable by ordinary beings.

Scrappy had the "it" factor.

Throughout Scrappy's tenure as a pet therapy dog, the foundation for the hospital where Scrappy worked had a very special fundraiser. Broadway performers brought their beautiful voices to town to perform their renditions of Broadway musicals. Months prior to the show, auditions were held for local youths in hopes that they could be a part of the show as well. It was a terrific event showcasing talent both locally and from abroad that we would not ordinarily ever see in our area.

A small but critical part of the show was the introduction of a few of the pet therapy dogs that worked within the hospital system. It was a magical way to showcase the dogs, discuss their amazing work, and share their achievements with the audience. Scrappy was fortunate enough to have been invited.

The day of the performance, we were asked to arrive at the theater several hours in advance of the show. However, we were not given much instruction. We had a program, so we knew the song when we were to walk out onto the stage, but that was about it. Patiently, we waited and waited and waited a little longer. Scrappy and the other dogs slept while performers walked by, sang, then exited stage right. The only stage fright these pet therapy dogs exhibited was when we had to wake them up.

Finally, we were getting close to our song. We got our cue and with the dogs on leashes, we entered the stage to see all the children who successfully made their auditions sitting randomly around the stage. Scrappy walked out, observed the children, made her way through a few of them to say hello, then discovered the front of the stage with hundreds of people in the audience watching. Scrappy was *on*. It was time for her to perform.

With what must have seemed to Scrappy like the world watching, she immediately pranced to the front of the stage, her tail wagging and made her presence known to everyone in attendance. She stood right next to the Broadway star who was leading that segment of the show, then glowingly sashayed down the length of the stage for all to see.

Was Scrappy supposed to do that? NO! But she took control of the room faster than a bolt of lightning. Scrappy had that "it" factor. In her own way, Scrappy was dancing with the music. A star was born.

She could see the audience smiling. She could hear the audience laughing. Within a few minutes, it was over, but Scrappy was a huge success and demonstrated why pet therapy dogs are so valuable to everyone they encounter. Pet therapy dogs provide an emotional release. They offer, to anyone watching, happiness—with zero effort. It is natural, and it is appealing to everyone.

Scrappy's fifteen minutes of fame were just beginning though.

After the show, the performers were back in their dressing rooms, refreshing themselves, taking pictures with VIPs, signing autographs, and the like. Scrappy and I went backstage to say goodbye to a few people when suddenly one of the performers grabbed my arm and asked if she could take a picture with Scrappy. Scrappy, that night, became a star of the stars.

And if that wasn't enough, we were then asked to join the stars of the show in the lobby of the theater to do a meet-and-greet with audience members. Scrappy was in her element. She had "it." I was simply her assistant and personal chauffeur.

Even after becoming a star, Scrappy always stayed true to herself. She did not have to be loud, she did not have to be announced. Scrappy never exhibited any airs. She was comfortable with herself and confident enough to show her personal strength.

When controlling the room, keep your head high, always looking forward, demonstrating your personal confidence. It is not necessary to be loud. It is not necessary to be obnoxious. What controlling the room does require is inner personal strength. Be true to yourself as Scrappy would.

The Last Act

Sunday, June 30, 2019, was the worst day of my life. That was the day little Scrappy left my physical world for a less painful spiritual word. In this world, she is playing with new friends and being held by my father, whom she loved greatly.

I believe Scrappy continues to watch me. I believe she knows when my emotions are brought to tears. I believe she is waiting for me and will continue to wait for me. She will be running to me at full speed when my last act concludes.

I believe all these things because, for one, we need to believe. Belief provides the eternal strength to continue. It provides emotional strength when we need it most, and it offers signs that we are being watched over, signs that someone is waiting for us.

I believe that Scrappy has given me signs that she is OK in her new spiritual world. After her passing, I had Scrappy cremated. While we were waiting for the cremation to be completed, Susie and I were home, trying to keep ourselves occupied. Our hearts were feeling pain unknown to us before. We needed a distraction. We were making up the bed together, and as I pulled the comforter to the top of the bed, a single piece of kibble appeared.

How did it get there? Scrappy never ate in bed. Her food was always downstairs. There was no explanation for it being there, and yet there it was. In my mind, there is only one explanation—Scrappy gave me a sign to assure me she was OK. This singular piece of kibble was her way of letting me know everything with her was alright, that her soul was in heaven. Her soul was at peace.

I took that singular piece of kibble and placed it in the container that holds a portion of Scrappy's ashes that I keep on my desk. The kibble went in first, then Scrappy's ashes. That singular piece of kibble is especially important to me, because it was the first sign I believe Scrappy has given me.

A week or so after Scrappy's passing, we played golf with friends— or at least attempted to. It was still too early for me. My heart and thoughts were still on Scrappy. In addition, it was on a Sunday. Scrappy passed on a Sunday, and that day of the week was now painful. Sundays were the worst day of the week for me; they could no longer make me happy. Somehow, Scrappy must have seen my pain from heaven.

We placed the majority of Scrappy's ashes in a beautiful wood vase that had been hand turned and carved by a friend of mine. However, it came without a top. So, when we placed Scrappy's ashes into the container, I used a small glass bowl that fit perfectly over the opening of the vase and provided the closure necessary.

The glass bowl was a gift to me from a client. She made the bowl herself. It was colorful, delicate—just like Scrappy—and the main detail of the bowl was a dragonfly. The dragonfly covered the bottom of the bowl and was the focal point of the art.

Why am I deviating from golf to a dragonfly? Because the dragonfly in the bowl became a sign from Scrappy that Sunday during golf.

As painful as golf was that Sunday, it did not compare to the pain I was feeling without Scrappy. After all, Sundays were incredibly special for Scrappy and me. Sundays were the days we went to parks to run and play. Sundays were the days nothing else was ever scheduled. The only commitments we had were to each other.

But this Sunday was miserable. Eighteen holes of golf can be taxing for time, energy, and a cause of frustration. I was experiencing all of those, with the loss of Scrappy on top of all of that. Then, out of nowhere, on the eighteenth hole, a dragonfly appeared. A large dragonfly, just like the figure in the bowl used to cover the vase holding Scrappy's ashes.

I believe Scrappy delivered that dragonfly intentionally. Afterall, we were playing golf with Jackson's parents who had come with Jackson to comfort Susie and me after Scrappy's passing. Scrappy did not permit many people to hold her, but this couple was the exception.

Scrappy loved these people. Her love for them was as obvious as Scrappy's love for me.

I believe Scrappy delivered this dragonfly to remind me everything is OK. This dragonfly, from the bowl that covered her ashes, hovered between me, Susie, and our friends. My emotions were brought to tears. I looked down to dry my eyes with my shirt, then looked up to see the dragonfly again, but it was gone.

In that short amount of time, my emotional pain disappeared. Do not get me wrong, I was still mourning—my emotions throughout the day had been extreme. Continuous tears and silence were all that could be heard from me during golf. But now, after the dragonfly, I was a little more calm. Somehow, I felt a little bit better. And I believe—no, I *know*—that Scrappy sent that dragonfly for me.

There have been multiple signs, I believe, that Scrappy has offered me. The last one I will mention involves a rabbit.

For weeks after Scrappy's passing, I would venture out onto the deck of our home and stare into the now-empty backyard. Before Scrappy's passing, the yard was never empty. It was our daily routine to go out and allow Scrappy time to bark, play, and in general just be silly. It was a great end to the business day.

But that was over, now. The yard was quiet, uneventful, and empty. It was painful. But I would go out every afternoon anyway, to stare at the empty yard and conjure up mental images of Scrappy playing. It was another emotion that brought me to tears.

After months and months of repeating this routine, off in the distance of the yard, in the back corner, I saw a rabbit. The rabbit was not doing anything special. It was just a rabbit, eating the clover in the yard. But from then on, the rabbit was there every day I walked out. I would just stare at it in the distance, and think about Scrappy.

Then one day, the rabbit was not in the back corner of the yard. It was close to the house, within ten yards of the house. As I gazed over the railing to watch my new little friend, the rabbit sat up on its hind legs and began cleaning its face with its paws, just as Scrappy would do after every meal.

Once again, my emotions were brought to tears, but my heart was a little calmer.

Scrappy brought great pleasure to so many people. Some she knew, and many others were complete strangers. But more than anyone else, Scrappy made *my* life better. She gave me guidance, comfort, and happiness. With Scrappy, I had a role in life greater than just my life. I had a purpose.

Many people would suggest that good people do good things. That may be true, but I believe Scrappy enhanced those traits for me. She had no reason to do the good things she did, other than the fact that she was a great dog. She instinctively had those traits. They did not have to be developed; they came naturally for Scrappy.

Life without Scrappy is not normal. When I need Scrappy the most, I look for those signs. Those signs can remove the pain and sorrow and replace them with warmth and comfort. We may not always see them right away. They may not be obvious. But I believe that, in time, when we reflect, we may remember a moment, an instance that reassures us that our loved one is still with us, spiritually. That is what love does. When your commitment is so strong to another being, I believe the passed person continues to be there for you.

I can no longer touch Scrappy. I only have mental images, memories of our time together. But our last moments together were powerful. Our last memories together were meaningful. Our time together had purpose.

Faith

What is faith?

We often think of faith in religious terms. We have faith in God. We have faith that God will protect us, guide us, give us wisdom, or whatever our request may be.

But how do we *define* faith? How do we know if we are faithful?

Is faith cheering on our football team? Or is that simply "hope?"

Is faith practiced only on Sundays? Or is faith practiced every day of the week?

We are only humans. Our emotions get in the way sometimes. We are not perfect. We are constantly challenged in life, and when things do not go right for us and our lives are too painful, do we question our faith?

When I think about how faith impacted Scrappy, it is clear to me. I know she had faith in me. She depended on me. In the most simplistic terms, she knew I would hold her and softly rub her chest when she needed comforting. She knew I would feed her when she was hungry. She knew every afternoon after 4 o'clock, it was time to play in the yard, bark, and simply be a young puppy, regardless of her age.

But is that faith, or an expectation?

There is no question: some of Scrappy's happiest days were spent at the children's hospital. She would squeal with excitement, spin around in circles, and greet anyone who was entering or leaving the building. She understood her role. She had confidence in herself that she was about to do something good.

Within a few minutes after entering the hospital, "Scrappy!" could be heard in a child's voice. There was excitement on all parts. Often, I would release her leash to allow her to run to the voice. She was known in this building. She was loved in this building. Everyone knew the good work she did there.

These people had faith in Scrappy. There was an understanding. They all knew Scrappy was needed, because they knew Scrappy would make these children feel something they had not felt in a long time: joy, pleasure, happiness. It may have only been five minutes with each child, but it was five minutes of absolute perfection that Scrappy provided. And for that brief moment of time, no one other than Scrappy could do this for them.

There was one particular little boy we always seemed to meet in the lobby of the children's hospital. It was not by design; it was just fortunate timing, I guess. As soon as he saw Scrappy, he would drop his bags, coat, hat, or whatever he was carrying, yell to Scrappy, and run as fast as he could to her. Scrappy knew this child very well. There was always a little bit of caution for Scrappy with this little boy, since he tended to get "overly excited" and would place his hands too firmly around Scrappy's little head. But with the patience and kindness only Scrappy could provide, she accepted his ambitious love. And without fail, the little boy—with both hands securely around Scrappy's head—would put his nose directly on Scrappy's nose. And without fail, Scrappy would allow this to happen for about two seconds—and would then proceed to lick the boy directly on his mouth! As soon as Scrappy licked him, the hands would come off her head and the little boy would back up, laughing. It was all Scrappy needed. She got the relief she wanted by going to her automatic defense mechanism of licking him in the mouth. The little boy got what he wanted: love from Scrappy, all while laughing enthusiastically. That love and happiness was something he had been missing since the last time he had seen Scrappy.

Scrappy had faith she was not going to be hurt, but that did not keep her from having some doubts. Regardless, she understood the boy, and the boy understood Scrappy. There was equal faith.

But it was not just the children. The doctors and nurses all knew Scrappy. They each took their time with Scrappy, too. These professionals are under constant stress. Lives are dependent upon their decisions. One wrong thought, decision, or action could be disastrous. Without question, their faith in themselves had to be a struggle at times. Scrappy allowed them to escape the pressure, escape any doubt in their own faith, even if for just a moment. Scrappy provided that release, provided one mental break to breathe again with confidence. They were witness to the healing powers of Scrappy. Now it was their turn to provide their own healing powers to the children, their patients.

Faith is hard to measure. Faith is hard to quantify. Faith is complex.

Scrappy had unmeasurable faith in me. All five pounds of her body was full of faith in me. She was dedicated to me, and I to her. It was understood on all levels. More faith in each other could not occur.

During pet therapy training, the most difficult test for Scrappy was called "separation." Someone, a stranger, had to hold Scrappy while I had left the room, completely out of sight, for three to five minutes. While I was gone, Scrappy could not bark, squirm, or try to separate from the stranger holding her. This was the only pet therapy test we ever had to practice.

As much as I wanted to sneak a peek, I knew I could not. I knew Scrappy watched me intensely as I left the room, but Scrappy had faith. She knew I would return. And when I did, her excitement could not be contained. The stranger holding her put her on the floor and, like a cartoon character, her little feet were moving on the vinyl floor to get traction, but nothing was happening. Then, all of sudden, the bottoms of her feet gripped the floor. She rocketed to me and jumped into my arms. She licked my face, squealed to let me know she loved me, then suddenly relaxed on my forearm and nestled her back on my bicep. I carried her to our seat as she proudly sat on my arm. I am not sure which was greater—her love for me or mine for her. I knew she would succeed, and she knew I would return. We had faith in each other.

Faith can be both a noun and a verb. As a noun, faith is devotional. When you have faith, you have dedicated your love, your all-encompassing being to someone else without remorse or hesitation.

As a verb, faith is alive. Faith has emotions that come to our mortal surface and are visible for all to see. Most importantly, faith is practiced. Faith is nothing more than hope, if it is not practiced.

Faith is an assurance—there is no higher connection. It is emotional. It is soulful. With faith, you have dedicated your total soul.

Scrappy had faith in me, even when she was her sickest. She knew I would make the right decision—as hard as it was. She knew that when our eyes locked onto each other and I could see her life fading, she knew I understood. She had faith in me to make the right decision for her, as I had done her entire life.

Her faith in me was comforting. My decision was painful. I made her live too long—I was the selfish one, and yet she still had faith in me.

She was calm. She was still. Life had been good, but was finally over. She had fulfilled her mission.

We went into the chapel at the children's hospital on our last day together. We sat in the front row, where I selfishly prayed for myself.

I knew what I was about to do, and my heart was in pain. And the entire time, Scrappy laid in my arms. She never moved. She never made a sound. She was practicing her faith. She understood me. She understood my pain. And yet somehow, she knew we were about to be separated.

I was beginning to question my faith. I knew I would miss her terribly. I was the one in pain, now. Where was my faith? When will my pain end? How long do I have to wait? When will I be reunited with Scrappy?

Scrappy had done so much with her life and honestly, I was afraid to move forward with my life without her. June 30, 2019 was a Sunday, our holy day, our day to be together. And the most cherished piece of my life was going to be taken away from me. Why?

It was not fair; it was not right.

Or was it?

Sundays are when we worship to demonstrate our faith. That day, of all days, is when Scrappy demonstrated her faith in me the most, to make a difficult decision and separate our physical lives from each other. No more kisses. No more nips of my nose. No more rubbing her chest. Worst of all, no more sitting on my left forearm.

When I notified my friends of Scrappy's passing, I sent a singular text: "My left arm is empty." Everyone who knew us understood the message immediately. There was no questioning, there was no misunderstanding. It was clear. They knew my heart was broken. They knew it would not be easily repaired.

Scrappy's life ended on a Sunday, our day of worship. As much as I questioned my faith on that day, maybe no other day would have been more appropriate for her to pass.

If Sunday is our day of faith, it is only appropriate for the greatest of souls to be received by God on His day. Scrappy, her entire life, showed her faith in me—all the way to her last day in this physical world. Now, she is in the eternal world, watching over me. She feels better, but I know she is lonely, she misses me. But as she always did, in my absence, she is patiently waiting for me to return. She has faith I will return, just as she did on that pet therapy test when I had to leave her in the room being held by a stranger. She had faith we would be reunited. And one day, we will. That will be the greatest day of my life.

As I laid her down on her bed for the last time, I placed my head over hers. I was sobbing relentlessly. I repeatedly told her, "I'm so sorry." But Scrappy retained her confidence in me as I made the worst decision I ever had to make. She had faith.

Scrappy knew what I was doing was painful for me, but had faith. She knew that my painful decision was removing her physical pain— something she needed. She had faith in me to do the right thing.

She knew I saw her getting weaker. She knew we had done all we could do for her. There was just one thing left to do, and she knew my decision was going to be the right one.

Faith is a collective emotional bond. It is reassuring, it is confidence, it is an attitude and an understanding.

Faith should be the way we live our lives. It should be how we practice life.

For those of us who knew Scrappy and loved Scrappy, she would want us to continue to live, to continue being human, and to grow to be remembered for how we lived, not how we died. She has faith in us, and we should live up to that faith.

I Choose to Remember

Scrappy taught me so much. Unfortunately, I did not necessarily realize how much she taught me until after she passed. I had to take the time to reflect on our lives together to truly understand. I would like to think that I already had many of the traits in me that I have discussed—like treating love as a responsibility, "licking the bowl," and having faith. But I strongly believe Scrappy made all those traits in me better. When I witnessed the good she did for those children, when I witnessed the smiles of passengers in the car next to us, when I witnessed the sincerity of the hugs given to Scrappy from those who needed something to hold, I know Scrappy was indeed the most special dog I will ever encounter.

Too often, when a life is removed from us, our memories of that life fade in frequency over time. Our memories do not go away; instead, they just do not come to us as often. It is not that we do not miss that life—we miss that life terribly. Instead, our lives have continued to move forward, whether we like it or not. But when we slow down and take the time to reflect and remember, the stories come roaring back to us. Remembering makes me sad because I miss Scrappy. But remembering makes me smile a little, dry my tears, and reminds me that I need to be as good as Scrappy as much as possible.

I remember when Scrappy got into pet therapy training. I just knew in my heart, Scrappy would be perfect—and she was. I learned about pet therapy from a neighbor who had gone through the training with her dog. I got the information, and off Scrappy and I went.

The first day of training was the best. After all the dogs sniffed each other and said hello, a large circle was formed with the dogs and handlers. Scrappy and I were in our place and then the largest dog in the class sat next to us, a beautiful smoke-gray Great Dane. He was still a puppy in age like Scrappy, just about 120 pounds larger than Scrappy.

Scrappy was smitten! She cozied up to this Great Dane immediately and would not leave his side unless it was our turn to perform the required training task. Once complete, Scrappy raced back to the Dane's hip, looked up for approval, and he looked down with a smiling face.

Two animals could not have ever been so different and yet so similar.

I remember when Scrappy gained one pound of weight. That does not sound like much to you or me, but when you start at five pounds, a one-pound gain is also a 20 percent increase in body weight. And it does not matter if you're a dog or human, a 20 percent increase is never good.

How did this happen? I blame it on treats. Scrappy and I had recently been introduced to a wonderful lady who graciously accepted us both. As the saying goes, the way to a man's heart is through his stomach, and she took the same approach with Scrappy...and with me. Even though this method was not necessary for either of us, it worked. And together, Scrappy and I had to lose a few pounds. It was easy for Scrappy, but not so much for me.

I remember bath time for Scrappy. Scrappy hated bath time. She did not like getting wet. I have witnessed Scrappy jump over a two-inch wide, one-millimeter-deep, wet surface to avoid getting her feet wet.

Bath time was never an enjoyable time for Scrappy, but she always overcame her fear. She was smart enough to know that when I took her collar off, something was up. Her beautiful face would turn sad and concerned. Her pace of energy slowed to a crawl, and she would try to disappear.

As I began running the water to a temperature I thought she would enjoy, Scrappy would slowly, very slowly, enter the bathroom, place herself next to my leg, and give in to the eventual suffering that was about to occur. She was so cute.

Once the water reached a comfortable temperature, I would scrape Scrappy from my leg, gently place her under the faucet to get her wet, shampoo her, then rinse her. The entire process took less than five minutes to complete.

Next came the drying process. With the towel, I would dry her just enough to allow her to escape the misery of the bath. She would then run wildly through the house, jumping and spinning, demonstrating to me her freedom from the water. She was free!

But then came the hair dryer. I would place Scrappy on a towel and use a hair dryer for the remainder of the process. Patiently, Scrappy waited. When it was finally over, the energy of her five-pound body was the equivalent of a five-thousand-pound bull (if that's possible). Bath time being over was the most joyous event possible for Scrappy.

I remember the children's hospital calling me and asking if Scrappy could be part of a Halloween event. Each year, staff from various departments of the hospital would dress up and form a Trick-or-Treat venue for the children who would not be at home for Halloween. Without fail, one group of nurses would always dress up as characters from *The Wizard of Oz*. And without fail, Scrappy was always asked to be Toto (she was not identical to Toto, but she was pretty darn close). Scrappy never disappointed and even allowed Dorothy to hold her. Best of all, no costume was necessary for Scrappy!

I remember Scrappy loving to chase squirrels. In fact, Scrappy knew the word "squirrel" and every time I would say it, she became alert. Scrappy would look for that squirrel. If she saw it, she would get into predator position, crouching low to the ground, and then she'd jump into action, chasing the squirrel up a tree. She never would have caught a squirrel, and she never would have hurt a squirrel. It was nothing more than a frivolous activity she truly enjoyed.

Our house had woods in the back and, to my amazement one day, I saw an albino squirrel looking through the patio doors into our kitchen. The squirrel was absolutely beautiful. Solid white with pink eyes. Gorgeous!

The squirrel seemed very friendly, as if looking for a friend to play with, but if I got too close to the door it would scamper up the closest tree (only about ten feet away).

When I saw the squirrel for the first time, I called out to Scrappy. All I had to say was "Squirrel," and she came to attention. She saw the squirrel at the patio door, charged toward it, and crashed into the closed glass door. Fortunately, Scrappy was not hurt—maybe a little dazed and confused, but not hurt. The squirrel, of course, scampered up the tree and spun around with its head facing down.

Once Scrappy got the cobwebs out of her head from hitting the door, I opened the patio door and let Scrappy out. She immediately raced to the tree holding the squirrel and started barking at the squirrel. Believe it or not, the squirrel started barking back at her.

The squirrel even came lower down on the trunk of the tree as if to tease Scrappy, twitching its tail wildly as Scrappy barked. It was as if the squirrel knew Scrappy could not jump that high, but also as if the squirrel knew Scrappy would not hurt him.

Many times after this first encounter, the squirrel came back to the patio doors. Each time, I would stand by the door, yell, "Squirrel!" to Scrappy, and open the door as Scrappy got close. The squirrel would run up the tree, Scrappy would run out of the house to the tree, the squirrel would bark, Scrappy would bark, Scrappy would get bored, Scrappy would relieve herself in the grass, and finally she'd come back into the house, leaving the squirrel for another day.

This routine was a regular event for Scrappy. The squirrel and Scrappy truly loved each other, I believe. Their friendship also gave us something that we could entertain the children with at the hospital. If I felt a child was just having a really bad day, and they did not seem to be interested in Scrappy, I would yell, "Squirrel!" and point to the window for Scrappy. Each time Scrappy heard the word "squirrel," she would sit high on my arm, completely at attention, and stare out the window looking for that squirrel. The kids always thought that it was so funny, and it absolutely changed the attitude in the room from not-so-interested to distractingly funny—exactly what the kids needed.

I remember a trip Scrappy and I took to San Antonio, TX. It was a business trip for me, but we had some spare time and we went for a walk along a portion of the famous Riverwalk. As we were walking, I noticed a young lady ahead of us, a model, being photographed. We stopped and waited out of view of the photo before proceeding.

Then the photographer noticed Scrappy. As we walked toward the photographer, he asked if he could take some pictures of Scrappy. Of course, was the reply. He then instructed us to go back a bit and walk toward him. All the while, the camera was clicking. He was repositioning himself for the next shot.

"Would you move to the side, please?" he called.

I stopped, turned around to see what was behind us. There was nothing.

Then I heard, "No, you. Would you move to the side? I don't want you in the picture, just the dog."

Of course I wasn't insulted—though maybe I should have been! It was hilarious to me. Think about it. I was asked to move out of the picture and a professional model was asked to take a break, all because the cutest darn dog this photographer had ever seen was making her way down the Riverwalk of San Antonio, TX. It was as if he had just discovered the next super model. Her name was Scrappy, and she was on a leash. Too funny.

I remember the first time Scrappy ever went to the beach. We had been invited by friends to go to Hilton Head Island, South Carolina. We went out early in the morning because the regulations there mandated that dogs play on the beach only during certain hours of the day. Scrappy was on her leash, and her best buddy, Jackson, was showing us the way.

We crossed over from the grass onto the sand, and Scrappy slowed from a sprint to a crawl. She was not sure what was under her feet. But Jackson knew this beach. He saw Scrappy slow down, so he turned his head backward to look at Scrappy. It was as if he said to her, "It's okay, let's go." Scrappy responded to Jackson and off they went.

Scrappy got close to the water, but of course did not go in—she hated to get wet. But the sounds of the water, the smell of the ocean, and the feel of more solid sand under her feet delighted Scrappy to no end. I looked up and down the beach to see if there were any other dogs playing. There was not. I reached down, took off the leash and started running. Scrappy chased me, passed me, and just kept going. She finally slowed down and turned, and the biggest smile you could ever imagine on a dog was on Scrappy's face. She was having the time of her life!

I remember when my friend Sam asked me for a favor. Sam's "second mother" was the mother of a boy Sam grew up with in their neighborhood. As is often the case when children grow up together with someone in the neighborhood, the families had come together and built their own friendships. This boy's mother became Sam's second mother, and when she fell ill, Sam called me.

Sam's second mother had been admitted to the hospital with a terminal condition. Sam was distraught over her condition, but he knew there was a way he could make her feel better, even if it was for only a brief period of time.

Enter Scrappy. At Sam's request, we met the family in her hospital room. With Scrappy on my arm, in her right spot, we entered the room and pure excitement came upon Sam's second mother's face. Sam introduced us to the family and, just as if we were visiting the children's hospital, Sam's second mother reached for Scrappy, held her, and kissed her. Scrappy graciously accepted.

To this day, Sam reminds me of this story. He cries. I cry. Sam lost his second mother shortly after that visit, but the gratitude he continues to show to me for Scrappy's brief visit is beyond imaginable. Sam chooses to remember.

I choose to remember, but I also choose to cry. I do not care. I am not afraid to allow my emotions to come to tears. It makes me better. It makes me want to do better every day.

Scrappy will always be my "baby," my "pumpkin," my "monkey," and I will always remember her as a little puppy full of love for me and those close to me. I will always remember her running in the backyard or the park. I will always remember her sleeping against the back of my legs at night. I will always remember the night of June 30, 2019, when her eyes stared into mine and told me enough is enough—it is time to go to another world, without you.

Since Scrappy's passing, I have written notes to her and placed them with her ashes and that one singular piece of kibble. I continue to do it, but not at the frequency I did shortly after her passing. I have not forgotten, I have not moved on. If time heals all wounds, I do not know how much time will be needed for me. I suspect it will be when Scrappy is reunited with me, placed in her rightful spot—the forearm of my left arm—in a spiritual world.

Today, I feel very connected to Scrappy when I hear the song "Forever Young" sung by Rod Stewart and written by Bob Dylan. Even though the song was written for a human, it holds a special meaning to me as it relates to Scrappy. In her passing, I hope that the Lord is with her, watching her, keeping her young and warm. I also hope that together, they are watching over me, giving me the strength I need in Scrappy's absence.

Scrappy made me a better person because I could see in her the passion she had for life. Even though Scrappy was only five pounds, every ounce of her body was used to make life for everyone in her world worthwhile.

Twelve

Blessed Life

Often, we refer to a "blessed life" when someone passes away. We speak about the great things they did during their lifetime—philanthropy, family, business, etc. Accomplishment becomes synonymous with this person.

Scrappy was that way. Without her knowing, she brought greatness upon herself. She was the one the children's hospital would call when a child needed comfort.

Scrappy was the one who made everyone smile when she looked out the car window to the car next to us.

Scrappy was the one whose love came pouring out to you when you were lucky enough to hold her.

We all know people who had this effect. Somehow, this person simply had the ability to make things better when we were in their presence. It was natural for them. It was not constructed; it simply happened. And that was how Scrappy lived her life. There was no effort on her part. It was just part of her nature.

Scrappy lived a blessed life.

But a blessed life is not just about the past; it is also about the present. And in those terms, I am the one who had, and continues to have, a blessed life. How often, in one's lifetime, do you get the chance to witness a soul affect others in a manner that borders religious measures? If sainthood were possible for dogs, Scrappy would qualify. I was witness to all the wonders of Scrappy. I was the fortunate one. I lived the blessed life during Scrappy's lifetime.

I was there when children screaming in fear and pain would stop when they saw Scrappy. The tears would stop, they would reach to hold Scrappy, and when they did touch her, fear and pain disappeared. Life was not normal for them, but at least for that moment, life was no longer painful. I saw Scrappy provide them peace. I saw Scrappy provide them dignity again.

That is a blessed life, and I was witness to what it meant to the children, their families, and the doctors and nurses.

I would watch with joy when we stopped at a traffic light. Scrappy would sit up on my lap, put her front paws on the armrest of the car, and peer out the window toward the car next to us. Without fail, Scrappy would make that person smile, point their finger, and laugh. If children were in the backseat, they would wave and want to speak with Scrappy. Windows would roll down and ten-second conversations would begin about how cute Scrappy was. Her presence was simply enough to put our lives at ease, to generate comfort, and to warm hearts.

That is a blessed life, and I was fortunate enough to witness her powers.

I was witness to how Scrappy reacted when love was returned to her. Simply by holding her, gazing into her eyes, and rubbing her chest, Scrappy would gaze back into your eyes, plop her head against your chest, and let out a small but loving sigh of comfort to let you know how much she loved you. Whether it was me, a child at the hospital, or a complete stranger, the reaction was always the same. This was Scrappy's way of letting you know she was saying "I love you." It was not overly dramatic. Simplistic, yet so powerful. Scrappy understood the meaning of gestures and how the simplest gesture would make our lives better.

That is a blessed life, and I was lucky enough to share Scrappy's loving power.

I was also witness to Scrappy's youth, even as she aged. Scrappy loved to play in the yard or a park. She had a system for her play. If it was the yard, she would venture into what we called "the jungle," a heavily landscaped area where she would become visibly lost. We would hear her plow through the landscaping, but visibility was not possible. She would rumble through that area for a few minutes, then poke her head out so she could see us and we could see her. Then she was off again. When that area of land was conquered and secured, she would come out, move to a high point of the yard, and lay down in the cool grass proudly gazing over the yard as if she were a high princess. This was her land, and she proudly guarded it.

If we were in a park, Scrappy would race to one corner, sniff around until I caught up with her, then race to another corner and repeat. She would bark loudly so she could hear the echo of her own voice. She would spin around in circles and jump in the air with joy. She would chase me to get me engaged.

Scrappy lived a blessed life. She accomplished so much. She did so much for others. Her heart was for everyone—she did not deny anyone her attention or love.

There is no doubt that during Scrappy's twelve-and-a-half years of life, she did more for others than most people do in their entire adulthood. Scrappy came to me for reasons I will never completely understand, but I am grateful for all she gave me. I am blessed to have seen the even more powerful blessings she gave to others.

If living multiple lives or previous lives is possible, Scrappy must have done so. How else could she have known, in this lifetime, how to correct, protect, and remove pain if she had not done so already? Her emotions were unnatural, and yet natural. We never expected anything less from Scrappy but were always in awe of her as she did her work at the children's hospital.

Much like with Scrappy, we hold onto the memories of our loved ones to remind us what a "blessed life" means. In time, it is our duty to take those memories to use them for good, in order to live a blessed life in the present. It would serve no purpose to forget the memories or to live in solitude. That is not our role as humans. It is our role to share, educate, and love others in a manner that illustrates a blessed life. No two blessed lives are the same, and they will come to each of us at different times of our lives. We must be prepared and respond to the opportunity of living a blessed life.

It is important to have something consistent in our lives, but what do we do when it is gone?

When my father passed away, we placed his ashes at the Mountain Home VA Cemetery in Tennessee. Every possible Saturday, I go there to speak with Dad. Our history was for me to call him on Saturday mornings. While we talked, we would simultaneously watch fly fishing shows on TV. We did not say much to each other, but much was communicated. Now, on these Saturdays, I say a little and hear nothing back, but much is still communicated.

I also take my phone so my mother can FaceTime with Dad. I flip the camera so she can see his headstone. Her face grows a little redder, her eyes water a little, and her lips move but I hear nothing—although much is communicated. She is speaking to Dad. I do not know what she is saying. I do not need to know what she is saying—it is private. But it is important to her. It is part of her routine with Dad.

My challenge with this routine is that the cemetery is next to the park where Scrappy and I would play. It was her place to run and, most importantly, bark. She would spin around in circles full of joy, sprint to the next tree, turn around, look at me, bark, and expect me to run to her.

Now the park is empty. There is no more barking. My only communication is the memory. I can hear Scrappy bark in my mind. I can see Scrappy run in my mind. I can see myself pick her up and hold her when the exhaustion of play requires a hug of love and appreciation.

But now, there is no more communication. I must deal with this reality every Saturday. My consistency is gone. It has been replaced with memories. It is not the same, but it will have to do, it is all I have.

"Life can only be understood backwards; but it must be lived forwards."
—Søren Kierkegaard[2]

Touch is essential to life. When life can no longer be felt, touched, caressed, or rubbed, life is over.

I can no longer touch Scrappy. I cannot feel the soft hair of her chest. I cannot feel her nip my nose. I cannot feel her kiss my face. But in my mind, I see her run. In my mind, I see her caring for all those young children. Imagery is all I have now, and I must use it wisely.

For years, I held the memories of Scrappy for just what they were— memories. I cried, I missed her. I could not move on. It was not until I realized those memories had a deeper and more meaningful purpose that I could even consider moving on.

2 https://www.goodreads.com/
quotes/6812-life-can-only-be-understood-backwards-but-it-must-be#

Each June 30th, I automatically wake up at 3 am. No alarms. No bells. I roll over to the left side of the bed to see the memory of Scrappy's once beautiful, dark eyes that always said "I love you" gazing into mine. I leave the house with Scrappy's ashes and return to the park, the most significant location for me and Scrappy. I sit, holding Scrappy's ashes in my hands, waiting for the sun to rise to give me warmth, to make me smile, and to reassure me everything will be alright.

It is during this time when all my memories come flowing over me. It is during this time when my emotions bring me to tears.

It is during this time when I am reminded that love is a responsibility. Scrappy never had anything to prove. She had already won over everyone's heart. But her love continued until the last beat of her heart.

My time to mourn is finally over. It was a long and painful process, but I am now content knowing my life was blessed by an amazing "little girl," my "monkey face," my "pumpkin," my Scrappy. My blessed life is because of Scrappy and our time together, and it would be wrong of me to live anything other than a blessed life. Scrappy taught me better.

Now, now it is time to celebrate. Celebrate the life of a five-pound soul named Scrappy. I will celebrate with a smile every time I have a memory come to my heart. I will celebrate Scrappy's life with every tear I wipe off my face. I will celebrate Scrappy with the same pride of the mother who lost her son. I celebrate her life by continuing to live my life as Scrappy taught me. I will continue to celebrate Scrappy by telling her story of love.

Life is complicated. Life has a beginning and life has an end. It is how you conduct yourself in between that determines how you will be remembered.

Scrappy made her very small part of the world a better place.

Have we done the same?

As humans, we are far from perfect and that is OK. But, in my mind, Scrappy was nearly perfect. If we could adopt just a few of her principles, maybe our lives could be a little better and maybe, just maybe, our world could be a little better.

Thank you Scrappy. I love you. I miss you.

Life Lessons from Scrappy

For all of Scrappy's twelve and a half years, she amazed me with her love, humored me with her puppy full of life attitude, and demonstrated an extraordinary grace of life. She was my best friend for all of those years, and it is only fitting to remind all of us of her kindness and the life lessons only Scrappy could share.

Love is a responsibility. It is not enough to casually say "I love you." It must be said with intent, purpose, and direction. Caress the face of the one you love, stare into their eyes, and then say "I love you." Love must be intentional for it to truly be love. Love must be felt. Love is visible.

Love is that emotional state when nothing else matters. When in love, we have accepted love as a responsibility, a sobering responsibility to provide security, peace, and warmth to each other.

Scrappy's love for me was intentional. Her love for me was visible, and her love lasted for her lifetime. Love is not just a statement, it is an emotion. Scrappy was an emotional creature. She did not want to disappoint, and therefore, I believe, that is why her love was a responsibility.

Make your love a responsibility. Make your love visible. Make your love felt by whomever it may be directed toward.

Be on call. There are times when we must make ourselves available to others. There are times when we must forgo our own interests for the needs of someone else. When that time comes, be there. Hold that hand.

We should all be on call. We have a responsibility to each other. People need each other. Sometimes we need to reach out to someone special, someone we trust. If you are that someone, be on call, be available, and be proactive in making sure those you love are safe. We never know the severity of the situation, but we should never back down from the responsibility. It is that important.

Scrappy taught me that being on call means you are the most important person in the world at that time. No one else can deliver the necessary strength you can. Being on call means you alone mean more to whoever needs you than anyone else in the world. Being on call means you have meaning and you have purpose. Use it.

Lick the bowl. Dogs lick the bowl because they are happy—they hunger for more. As humans, we need to lick the bowl and then go back for more. Happiness is essential for all beings. It can come in different forms—whether physical or emotional. Happiness is a choice; it is an acceptance of our desire to reach a higher level of life. Happiness is our ability to lick the bowl.

But happiness must be sought out. It is not a given that happiness will prevail. We must work hard to be happy. We must surround ourselves with the right people in order to be happy.

We all have people in our lives who simply make us feel differently than other people. Our heart feels a little different in their presence. Our step is a little faster in their presence. Let them know this. Find a way to make your happiness visible so someone else understands their importance to you.

Take time to bring your emotions to tears. Do not be afraid to cry. There is strength in crying. There is purpose in crying. When we bring our emotions to tears, it shows we care. It shows we are devoted to a cause or a person of significance in our lives.

Tears do not have to come from a place of sadness. Tears can also come from a sense of pride. The greatest title I will ever own is "Scrappy's dad." Nothing makes me prouder than that.

But Scrappy also taught me to take time—the first two words of the title of this chapter. If we do not take time, we do not have the ability to reflect. If we do not take time, we do not have the ability to pause. If we do not take time, we do not have the ability to move forward with purpose.

Make a difference with your life. Make it impactful on others. When done, I promise you, you will be able to bring your emotions to tears. Those tears will make you stronger for the rest of your life.

Be more than a pet. Scrappy was never just a pet. She was my companion, my best friend. We traveled together. We explored the country together. We learned together. Scrappy taught me that we must get out of the house, get out of our areas of comfort in order to grow mentally and mature. Experience new people, experience new cultures, experience new places. Life is full of opportunity. It is our responsibility to seek it.

Wag your tail. Friends are one of the most valuable assets we have in life. Friends make us happy and keep us "in line" when we stray. Scrappy taught me that we may not always know our personal value, but there is always someone out there who values us personally.

Scrappy taught me that we cannot be *friends* with everyone, but what we can do is be *friendly* with everyone. Being friendly does not take effort. Being friendly to everyone would make our world a better place.

Much like Scrappy taught me love is a responsibility, so is friendship. Friends do not have to come in quantity, but friends do need to come in quality. We may be happy to see a thousand people, but only a few will we call our friends. These are the ones we love to see. These are the ones that we love. These few are the ones who will make your tail wag.

Find the right spot. We all have a place or a person that makes us feel something great no one else can. The right spot is where we find peace. The right spot is where we are soothed to a point of complete relaxation.

Scrappy taught me that the right spot is where we can ease the challenges of our day. The right spot is that person who makes us smile, makes us laugh. The right spot is where life slows so we can reflect and remember what is important to us. The right spot is where we feel we belong.

Finding the right spot is important because it must come from someone or something else—it cannot be duplicated by ourselves. As humans, we need to know we are appreciated. The right spot, for us, gives us comfort, but it can also give a feeling of gratitude or reward for doing a job well. The "right spot" reward motivates us to do it again and again with greater enthusiasm each time. Partners, significant others, spouses, or bosses all need to discover that right spot. It makes everyone feel better. It makes for greater achievements. It makes for better relationships.

Control the room. There are moments, particularly in business, when it's necessary to control the room. We must make an important statement that will impact everyone. In order to control the room, we must exude confidence.

Scrappy taught me that in order to control the room, we do not have to be loud. We do not have to be rude. Instead, we can simply be confident. We can allow the strength of our personalities to gain the respect of those we encounter each and every day.

The last act. Life presents challenges we must manage every day. Some challenges are easier than others, but regardless, decisions and actions are necessary.

Scrappy taught me that the last act may be difficult, but it should be memorable. The last act provides us an opportunity to remember why we love, why we need each other. The last act may be sad, but it may also be happy. It is up to us to decide which emotion we want to be left with.

We need to believe. Belief provides the eternal strength to continue. It provides emotional strength when we need it most, and it offers signs that we are being watched over, signs that someone is waiting for us.

Faith. Faith is both a noun and a verb. As a noun, faith allows us to hold something of value, something meaningful. As a verb, faith is actionable. Faith allows us to practice something we believe in.

We are only humans. Our emotions get in the way sometimes. We are not perfect. We are constantly challenged in life. And when things do not go right for us, when our lives are too painful without understandable reasons, do we question our faith?

Faith is hard to measure. Faith is hard to quantify. Faith is complex.

Scrappy taught me faith is an assurance. It is emotional. It is soulful. With faith you have dedicated your total soul. Scrappy demonstrated her faith in me every day, but especially on her last day. We can all follow her lead and show more faith in ourselves and in each other.

I choose to remember. Scrappy and I fostered endless memories together. It is important to remember. Memories are all we are left with when someone passes away. We can not forget; we must remember the past to make our futures liveable.

Scrappy taught me it's OK to remember, but it's also OK to cry. Do not be afraid to cry when you remember. Do not be afraid to bring your emotions to tears. Those same tears from those same memories will make you better, make you stronger.

Blessed life. We often refer to people who have passed as "living a blessed life." They accomplished many things. They emotionally touched many people. Their lives had an impact.

Scrappy taught me that someone may have lived a blessed life, but it is those who surrounded that life who are truly blessed. Scrappy was an amazing animal. She made everyone she spent time with better. She made them happier. She made them forget their problems and refocus on something good.

I was fortunate enough to witness Scrappy's impact on so many people. That made me a better person. It made me want to have the same impact as Scrappy. Scrappy made me want to be a better person every day.

Rainbow Bridge

Just this side of heaven is a place called Rainbow Bridge.
When an animal dies that has been especially close to
someone here, that pet goes to Rainbow Bridge. There
are meadows and hills for all of our special friends so
they can run and play together. There is plenty of food,
water, and sunshine, and our friends are warm
and comfortable.
All the animals who had been ill and old are restored to
health and vigor. Those who were hurt or maimed are made
whole and strong again, just as we remember them in our
dreams of days and times gone by. The animals are happy
and content, except for one small thing; they each miss
someone very special to them, who had to be left behind.
They all run and play together, but the day comes when
one suddenly stops and looks into the distance. His bright
eyes are intent. His eager body quivers. Suddenly he begins
to run from the group, flying over the green grass, his legs
carrying him faster and faster.
You have been spotted, and when you and your special friend
finally meet, you cling together in joyous reunion, never to
be parted again. The happy kisses rain upon your face; your
hands again caress the beloved head, and you look once more
into the trusting eyes of your pet, so long gone from your life
but never absent from your heart.
Then you cross the Rainbow Bridge together....

— Author Unknown[3]

[3] https://www.rainbowsbridge.com/poem.htm

Special Thanks

A Tail of Love: Life Lesson from Scrappy, a Pet Therapy Dog would not be possible if it were not for a large group of people, who loved Scrappy, and supported me during this endeavor. There are too many of you for me to mention here, but it is necessary for me to acknowledge a few that held my hand more than once.

Christina Bagni, Chief Editor, Wandering Words Media, took a mess of words and emotions, and molded them into a flowing, readable book. Without her understanding of my messages, a book never would have been published.

Lucy Holtsnider crafted the cover of the book into a beautiful representation of Scrappy. The leash, the heart, and the badge mean as much to me as the book itself. Find her complete portfolio at LucyHoltsnider.com.

It takes a lot of effort to convert emotions into words. And, at least for me, it requires a special place to pause and reflect in order to put those emotions into words.

In order for me to complete this book, a sanctuary of solitude, surrounded by the beauty of nature was absolutely necessary. Fortunately, there were two places that fit the bill:

<table>
<tr><td>Meredith Valley</td><td>Lindsay's Log House</td></tr>
<tr><td>Elizaethton, TN</td><td>Stillwater, NY</td></tr>
<tr><td>June 28, 2020</td><td>June 30, 2021</td></tr>
</table>

Without these incredibly beautiful homes in inspirational locations, my words would have taken even longer to complete.

Susie, what can I say other than what I have said time and time again? I provided Scrappy a house, but you gave her a home. WE love you!

Joy McCray, the one and only. My social media guru understands social media is not my skill-set, but taught me to do it anyway. Your patience with me is greater than anyone would ever understand. Your insight is beyond my comprehension. You kept telling me, "This is going to be great!"

Thank you to everyone who read this book prior to publication and encouraged me, focused me, and inspired me to write, write some more, and then write some more.

I would be remiss if I did not mention the professionals in the children's hospitals we visited. Scrappy and I admired your dedication to those children and their families. Your sincere devotion to improve the lives of those children is heroic.

Finally, thank you to everyone who knew and loved Scrappy. Scrappy will be forever in our hearts.

About the Author

Larry Grogan is an investment advisor by trade but an animal lover at heart. At an early age, Grogan and his father would go fishing together in the mountains of North Carolina, where part of the daily routine was to watch deer grazing in the meadows next to the trout stream. From that point on, the beauty of nature and its contents significantly impacted Larry's approach to life.

Much later in life came Scrappy. Scrappy was a five-pound mixture of Toy Poodle and Chihuahua, a close clone of Toto from *The Wizard of Oz*. A better soul could never have been created. When Scrappy passed away in 2019, writing became a method of therapy for Larry. Her absence in his life was immense, and it took over two years for Larry to complete his memoir of Scrappy.

Larry's first book, A *Tail of Love: Life Lessons from Scrappy, a Pet Therapy Dog* chronicles many of Scrappy and Larry's experiences together visiting children's hospitals and other healthcare facilities. Cancer, illness, assault were just a few of the painful tragedies these young people suffered. And through it all, Scrappy was able to comfort all of them, as well as their families, with grace and dignity.

For eight years Scrappy was a pet therapy dog. Through Scrappy, Larry was able to illustrate the positive impact pet therapy dogs have on patients. These experiences and observations changed Larry's life, and he hopes they may have a similar impact on your life.

"Wow, I have to be honest: this is one of my favorite books I've ever worked on. I don't think I've ever cried while editing before, but this book had me in tears several times. Really, really good work. I'm sure you've made Scrappy proud!"

—Christina Bagni, Chief Editor, Wandering Words Media

wanderingwordsmedia.comfacebook.com/
WanderingWordsMedia

Thank you for reading our book!

We really appreciate all your honest feedback and would love hearing what you have to say about our memoir.

Should we ever consider writing a sequel to *A Tail of Love: Life Lessons From Scrappy, a Pet Therapy Dog*, your input would be valuable to that process.

Finally, please provide an honest review on Amazon letting me know what you thought of the memoir.
Thank you very much!

If you would like to honor Scrappy or a pet that you love, please consider a donation to an animal charity or a children's hospital of your choice.

https://www.facebook.com/Scrappythepettherapydog

instagram.com/lifelessonsfromscrappy

larrygrogan5@gmail.com

Made in the USA
Columbia, SC
26 July 2022

64042811R00076